Documentation Development Methodology

Techniques for Improved Communications

SANDRA PAKIN AND ASSOCIATES, INC.

PRENTICE-HALL, INC.
Englewood Cliffs, New Jersey 07632

Library of Congress Cataloging in Publication Data
Main entry under title:

Documentation development methodology.

Includes index.
1. Electronic data processing documentation.
2. Report writing. 1. Sandra Pakin & Associates.
II. Title.
QA76.9.D6D6 1984   808′.066001   83-13674
ISBN 0-13-217167-8

QA
76.9
·D6
D6
1984

Editorial/production supervision: Nancy Milnamow
Manufacturing buyer: Gordon Osbourne

This 1984 edition is published by
Prentice-Hall, Inc., Englewood Cliffs, New Jersey 07632

Printed in the United States of America

10 9 8 7 6 5 4 3 2 1

ISBN 0-13-217167-8

Prentice-Hall International, Inc., *London*
Prentice-Hall of Australia Pty. Limited, *Sydney*
Editora Prentice-Hall do Brasil, Ltda., *Rio de Janeiro*
Prentice-Hall of Canada Inc., *Toronto*
Prentice-Hall of India Private Limited, *New Delhi*
Prentice-Hall of Japan, Inc., *Tokyo*
Prentice-Hall of Southeast Asia Pte. Ltd. *Singapore*
Whitehall Books Limited, *Wellington, New Zealand*

Table of Contents

Illustration List

 **Preface**

Computer system and application documentation rarely satisfies its readers. They find it difficult to read, too complicated, full of unnecessary information while lacking necessary information, and boring. The root of the problem is the traditional approach to documentation development, where analysts or programmers prepare the documentation as an afterthought to their other system development responsibilities.

Analysts, programmers, and other management information systems (MIS) professionals are not trained in documentation development in the same way they are trained in system development. Rather, the assumption is that speaking the language and knowing the subject matter are the only prerequisites to writing documentation. This is a misconception. Documentation development is a learned skill that improves with practice.

MIS professionals can produce effective documentation by following the Documentation Development Methodology (DDM).

ABOUT THE DDM   Created by Sandra Pakin & Associates, Inc. (SP&A) for use in its client engagements, the DDM is a proven approach for developing all types of formal written materials. It consists of ten tasks that structure the documentation development process into containable units of work beginning with planning and following through with writing, critical reviews of the writing, graphic development, and production coordination. Each DDM task has a definite product and builds on the output of the previous task.

The DDM is a methodology for people committed to producing good documentation. Those looking for a quick-and-dirty way to meet a documentation obligation will find that the DDM is not for them. Producing good documentation is hard work, just as producing a good computer system is hard work. The purpose of the DDM is to give that work structure and direction, to ensure that the right documentation is being produced for the right audiences.

ABOUT THIS BOOK   *DDM: The Documentation Development Methodology* explains the DDM and provides the background necessary to perform the DDM tasks. It is not a traditional writing textbook. It assumes that you know the rudiments of grammar, English syntax, and punctuation. It also assumes that you are working in a professional data processing or MIS environment, have something of substance to write, and are looking for a way to improve your documentation.

DDM: The Documentation Development Methodology is not intended to turn you into a professional writer. Instead, it is designed to show that you can produce clear, understandable materials if you:

- Plan your documentation.
- Seek reviewer support.
- Take the time to rewrite.
- Use a graphic approach.

To demonstrate the practicality of the DDM, the book uses examples and illustrations from all types of MIS documents. However, its major emphasis is on producing manuals.

CONTENTS The book contains sixteen chapters divided into six parts. Part 1 is the keystone for the book. It provides the whats and whys of the DDM. The remaining parts are organized *by function* and concentrate on the how-tos for the various documentation skills needed to produce good documentation.

Part 1, "The DDM," discusses the elements of good documentation so you understand the documentation goal you are trying to achieve. It then summarizes the DDM tasks and explains how you use the DDM for your documentation projects.

Part 2, "Planning," discusses how to structure a documentation project, how to plan a document, and how to prepare for production.

Part 3, "Review," describes how to identify reviewers, set review goals, and conduct reviews, so you are able to improve your documentation through properly managed reviews.

Part 4, "Writing," explains how to transform your plan into text, then how to refine your first draft into an effective piece of writing, and finally how to prepare reference aids.

Part 5, "Graphics," discusses page format and layout, text and graphic standards, and development of figures and illustrations.

Part 6, "Production," discusses production control, support services such as word processing, production methods for page preparation and reproduction, and project wrap-up.

The Reference section contains a sample project plan, a sample project writing guide, a list of additional readings on relevant writing topics, a glossary, and an index.

If you apply the principles discussed in *DDM: The Documentation Development Methodology,* you should be able to develop documentation that is recognizably better than anything you have previously written. You should also have increased confidence in your ability to develop good documentation and a basis for continued improvement of your documentation skills.

 **Part 1**
The DDM

If you do high quality work, you should be sure that your documentation does your work justice.

Good documentation is the result of:
- Effective planning, good writing, and careful review and production.
- Knowing the audience and including the information they need to understand the documentation.
- Incorporating the elements that make good documentation.

The Documentation Development Methodology (DDM) provides a documentation framework so all writers — professional and non-professional — can produce good documentation. This part discusses the elements of good documentation, defines the DDM, and describes how it is used. The remaining parts detail the planning, review, writing, graphics, and production skills needed to produce good documentation.

The chapters in this part are:

Chapter 1 - Elements of Good Documentation
Before you can use the DDM successfully in your documentation projects, you should understand your goal. You should know what makes good documentation. This chapter discusses how right choices of medium, language, visuals, and reference aids produce good documentation.

Chapter 2 - DDM Structure
The DDM consists of ten tasks which structure the development of good documentation. This chapter summarizes the DDM tasks.

Chapter 3 - Using the DDM
The DDM works for both small and large documentation projects. This chapter shows how to tailor the DDM tasks for projects of various sizes. It also discusses support services for documentation development, project management, and the integration of DDM tasks with your other work.

Chapter 1
Elements of Good Documentation

Chapter 1
Elements of Good Documentation

All of us have, on occasion, read good documentation. It was easy to understand and easy to use. It looked good.

Good documentation is no accident. It results from making a series of good choices. This chapter discusses some of the choices you must make to produce good documentation:

- Media
- Language
- Appearance
- Reference aids

The next two chapters discuss how the Documentation Development Methodology provides a framework for making these choices.

Deciding on the Proper Media

Manuals are the mainstay of documentation. However, other presentation alternatives exist — for example, brochures, reference cards, and help screens. These should be considered along with manuals when you are planning the best presentation for reader understanding. Good documentation starts with the proper media selections so that you are not trying to accomplish all your documentation goals with a single document.

MANUALS Manuals should answer most of a reader's questions and all of the common ones. Manuals provide the most convenient format for complete information on a topic; however, they should direct that information to specific audiences or should cover specific functions.

Often the best way to make the information appropriately specific is to design the manuals in modules, where each module is a discrete content unit of information. Various combinations of modules form manuals tailored to meet the unique needs of each audience. For example:

- Data entry operators receive a module explaining how to use the terminal, plus a module of detailed entry procedures for each application they use. Thus, each operator's manual, when assembled, contains only those modules needed by that operator.
- Lead operators or supervisors receive the data entry operator modules plus an additional module on batch control procedures and file maintenance.

- Managers and general user groups get a system overview module, modules on interpreting reports for applications they use, and possibly modules on terminal use and inquiry functions.

Choosing a modular approach to structuring manuals is a cost-effective and efficient method of supplying information. No one receives unnecessary documentation, and modules satisfying various audiences can be widely distributed.

BROCHURES

If you have training classes planned and a user's guide prepared, you are ready to present the system in detail. But no training class or reference manual — however well done — can make a new system seem easy to use. The information required to cover every operational detail clouds the underlying simplicity of the system. To snapshot their systems, vendors use brochures. The brochure works similarly to ensure acceptance of in-house systems.

A brochure can be the appropriate documentation choice for top management, for example. Manuals provide too much detail-oriented information and do not cover the benefits of the system from a management perspective.

Well laid out in easy-to-use form, a brochure transmits high-level information in a few pages. The brochure tells users what to expect of the system. It shows the reader that the main system features and operations are simple enough to be explained in four-to-eight pages.

REFERENCE
SUMMARY CARDS

After readers are familiar with the information in a manual or have attended a training class, they may need a quick review of a specific procedure. The reference summary card is a way to refresh memories. Reference summary cards are useful in situations like the following:

- A minicomputer system operator needs a step-by-step restart/recovery procedure.
- A salesman in the field who uses a touch-tone system for calling in sales orders directly to a computer system needs the calling procedure and codes.
- Management needs instructions on using an online inquiry system to preview financial reports.

The reference summary card can be a one- or two-sided card to post over a desk or slide under a terminal keyboard, or it can be a fanfold which fits into a pocket. It should present one subject, one set of related procedures. It should serve one audience.

HELP SCREENS

Help screens supplement a reference manual by providing specific reference information to the online user. It is very convenient for the user to call up information about a screen at the time he is using the screen. This often saves time and improves user efficiency. Help screens are user or operator documentation. To be effective, they should employ the elements of good documentation.

Using Suitable Language

Good documentation shows effective language choices. This means it uses words readers know and has short, direct sentences and paragraphs.

™ of Sandra Pakin & Associates, Inc.

VOCABULARY When a choice exists, the writer who is striving for understanding selects the common word. He writes *find out* instead of *ascertain, ended* instead of *culminated,* and *based on* instead of *predicated on.* He defines all abbreviations, acronyms, and symbols the first time he uses them and includes system and business terms in a glossary.

The writer who is striving for readability selects short words. He writes *before* instead of *prior to, also* instead of *in addition to,* and *show* instead of *demonstrate.*

The writer who is communicating with a non-technical audience avoids technical terminology whenever possible. He writes *enter* instead of *input, report* instead of *hardcopy,* and *type* instead of *key.* But when it is important that the reader learn a technical term, the writer provides a definition written in language the reader understands.

SENTENCE AND PARAGRAPH STRUCTURE Sentence structure, or syntax, is the way words are put together to form thoughts. The most readable sentences are short, 18 to 25 words per sentence for business writing. They rarely contain semicolons, colons, or remarks in parentheses. They are action-oriented and contain only the words needed to express the thought.

Paragraphs should be short, averaging 75 words per paragraph. Occasionally, a single-sentence paragraph is desirable to change the pace or to emphasize an important point. But having too many single-sentence paragraphs means failure to tie thoughts together.

Within a paragraph, the topic sentence usually comes first, followed by sentences that support the point of the topic sentence. There are many ways of presenting supporting information. For example, bulleted or numbered lists can be used to highlight key information, and charts can consolidate information to show similarities and differences.

Making an Effective Appearance

We are living in a visual age. Television, newspapers, magazines, even textbooks present ideas in diagrams and pictures. Emphasis on visuals is particularly needed for materials aimed at non-technical audiences.

Studies indicate that readership goes down when the material looks too long or too difficult. Directing the material to a specific audience or specific function helps contain the size of a manual.

Using graphics makes the material easier to understand. This does not mean you must turn your documentation into comic books. You prepare a well-designed page format and appropriate illustrations to improve reader comprehension.

PAGE FORMAT The visual impact of a page is an important factor in whether the page is read. Line after line of text filling the entire page is visually boring and implies the text itself is boring. The overall image of a page is relaxed when you combine blocks of text with headings and figures. Figure 1.1 illustrates this.

Three aspects of page format affect the appearance of the page: typography, white space, and consistency. In each of these areas, you must choose what is best for your material and audience. The goal is an easy movement of the eye through all the information on the page.

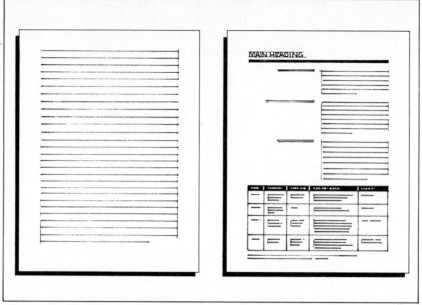

Figure 1.1 Varying the page elements. This makes the page visually more interesting.

Typography. The type should be large enough and simple enough to be easily read. It should not be all capital letters, italics, or OCR type. Line length should not exceed six inches. A four-inch line is easiest to read, according to legibility studies.

Special circumstances may affect your selection of type size. For example, materials used at a work station, such as operator instructions, may require a larger print than summary information read at a desk.

White space. White space on the page allows the reader's eye to rest. Adequate margins frame the text, make complex material appear less formidable, and highlight important features. For typed documents, variations of line spacing between paragraphs and subsections make text appear less monotonous than consistent doublespacing between lines.

Consistency. Varying format elements is distracting for the reader. Headings of similar importance in the text should be treated similarly. All illustrations of reports or display screens should have the same size reduction and use the same style of verbal and number callouts. Only one or two illustration widths should be used. Either the same amount of space or a line should delineate illustrations from the text.

EXAMPLES AND ILLUSTRATIONS
Examples and illustrations support and amplify verbal explanations. They help make concepts specific and show how things look and work. The writer determines when illustrations should be used and what type of illustrations improve the readability of the material.

For instance, many experienced readers can learn how to operate a system simply by working through a good set of examples and illustrations. Report and screen examples with actual data are harder to prepare but have more value to the reader. Also, when examples throughout a manual are related, the reader can follow the processing flow.

Illustrations of equipment, screens, and reports eliminate the need for narrative explanations of this visual information. Illustrations of processing flows clarify and codify interrelated processing or logic steps. These are essential illustrations in every user's or operator's guide.

Simply including examples and illustrations does not, however, improve documentation. To be effective, each illustration must be an essential piece of documentation — well planned, carefully prepared, properly labeled, and easily understood. The text should refer to the illustration specifically.

Providing Reference Aids

Most documentation is not meant to be read like a short story or novel. Instead, it is a reference — a source of vital information for weeks, months, and often years.

Reference aids — such as section and subject headings, tables of contents, glossaries, and indexes — are essential for good documentation. They make it easier for a reader to use and reuse a document because they help him find what he wants to know.

All types of documentation require headings to orient the reader to their content. Headings introduce and highlight key points. They help readers scan the text for information. To be useful in scanning, headings must be brief and understandable out of context. Most pages should have *at least* one heading, and the subordination of headings should be clear.

Besides headings, every manual requires a table of contents, glossary, and index:

- Table of contents — lists section titles and page numbers in the order in which they appear in the manual and shows the structure and organization of the manual. Any document over 25 pages should have a table of contents. Long documents may benefit from additional content listings at the beginning of each chapter.
- Glossary — provides an alphabetic listing, with definitions, of the unfamiliar and unique terms and abbreviations used in the manual.
- Index — provides an alphabetic listing of topics covered in the manual. The index gives page numbers for all references on a topic in one place so the reader can find all pertinent discussions in the manual.

Manuals of more than 25 pages may include the following additional reference aids:

- Illustration list — lists page numbers for figures, illustrations, and tables.
- Chapter tables of contents — precede each chapter's text to show detailed contents.
- Index tabs — divide the manual to make it easy to locate chapters or parts.
- Figure captions — identify each figure.
- Reference appendixes — list specialized information that the user needs to use the system, including error messages, special functions, and codes.

Checklist of Elements of Good Documentation

The elements of good documentation are identifiable and attainable by a series of good choices. In making a media choice, you consider how to present the information, choosing the form or format most effective for the material and the audience. In making language and appearance choices, you determine how to state, illustrate, and package the information so it is easy for the audience to use and understand. Finally, in providing reference aids, you make it easy for the reader to find the information he needs.

The following checklist can help you evaluate the quality and usability of your documentation.

MEDIA — Choosing the most effective form or format for the material based on the audience's information needs.

- ☐ Each presentation medium suits the purpose of the communication:
  - Reference and training — manual
  - Overview of application or system — brochure
  - Reference to specific information — reference card
  - Online assistance in using the system — help screen or tutorial.
- ☐ Each document has a specific audience or covers a specific function.

LANGUAGE — Making the information easy for the reader to use and understand.

- ☐ Common words are used.
- ☐ Abbreviations, acronyms, and symbols are explained.
- ☐ Technical terminology is avoided.
- ☐ Sentences are short, 18 to 25 words.
- ☐ Sentences rarely contain parenthetical remarks, semicolons, or colons.
- ☐ Paragraphs are short, averaging 75 words.
- ☐ Bulleted and numbered lists and charts occur where appropriate.
- ☐ Overly informal and patronizing language is avoided.

APPEARANCE — Making it easy for the reader to digest the material.

- ☐ Type is large enough to be read easily.
- ☐ All capital letters, italics, or OCR type is avoided.
- ☐ Text lines are no longer than six inches and are limited to four inches whenever possible.
- ☐ Margins frame the text and are wide enough to accommodate the binding.
- ☐ Illustrations are delineated from the text.
- ☐ Concepts are supported by specific examples.
- ☐ Equipment, screens, reports, and forms are illustrated.
- ☐ Actual data is included whenever possible to improve the effectiveness of illustrations and examples.
- ☐ Examples and illustrations are properly labeled and legible.
- ☐ Examples and illustrations are referenced from the text.

REFERENCE AIDS — Making it easy for the reader to find the information he needs.

- ☐ Headings introduce and highlight key points.
- ☐ Subordination of headings is clear.
- ☐ Table of contents shows chapters, sections, and subjects and includes page numbers.
- ☐ Glossary defines all business and system terms used in the manual.
- ☐ Index includes detailed entries.

Chapter 2

DDM Structure

Chapter 2
DDM Structure

Producing good documentation, like producing good systems, is not a haphazard process. It is a structured process that begins with planning and follows through with writing, illustrating, and producing the document. Review points are specified throughout the process to control the risk of producing unwanted, inaccurate, or ineffective materials.

The Documentation Development Methodology (DDM) provides a development framework for producing good documentation. It consists of ten tasks that divide the documentation development process into containable units of work.

This chapter describes each of the DDM tasks. Chapter 3, "Using the DDM," discusses how to tailor the DDM for documentation projects of varying sizes and how to integrate it into your work.

The Documentation Development Methodology

Figure 2.1 lists the ten tasks of the DDM. You perform the first task, Plan Documentation Project, for the documentation project as a whole. You perform the remaining tasks for each document in the project.

Each DDM task has a definite product and builds on the output of the previous task. This simplifies both planning of the development effort and fulfilling of development responsibilities. It also makes it easy to tailor the DDM for documentation projects of any size.

1 - Plan Documentation Project
2 - Plan Document Content
3 - Plan Document Format
4 - Review Document Plan and Commit to Writing
5 - Write First Draft
6 - Develop Graphics
7 - Review Technical Detail
8 - Rewrite and Complete Graphics
9 - Review Final Draft and Commit to Publication
10 - Coordinate Publication

Figure 2.1 DDM Tasks

The DDM emphasizes planning and review. Untrained writers often overlook document planning. They leap right into writing, believing they already know what they want to say. Writing without a document plan is like programming without a system design. It is inefficient and error-prone.

Before writing begins, you must complete the DDM's three planning tasks. The project plan identifies all the audiences requiring documentation and the appropriate document to meet each information need. When you plan the content and format for each document, you determine organization, appearance, and level of detail before you begin writing. This approach eliminates unnecessary and redundant development.

When your aim is good documentation, you also need reviews to check the material for accuracy and effectiveness *during development*. These reviews curtail the waste of time and resources involved in correcting poorly written or badly targeted materials.

The DDM's three review tasks occur at critical points in documentation development:

- When planning is complete but *before* writing begins, to confirm that the document plan reflects the objectives, organization, and content intended for the document.
- After a first draft is written, to confirm its technical accuracy and completeness.
- Before printing, to ensure the rewritten document is accurate, effective for the audience, and correctly assembled.

These reviews are essential. For some documents, particularly manuals, additional reviews may be necessary. The disciplines of planning and review and the refinement of the material based on review distinguish good from mediocre documentation.

DDM Task Descriptions

This section briefly explains each of the ten DDM tasks. The discussion previews the development accomplishments for each task and notes its output. Each development task builds on the output of the previous task to avoid redundant or repetitive effort. The diagram at the end of this chapter, Figure 2.2, illustrates the DDM processing flow and shows the outputs from the DDM tasks.

The DDM explanations assume a documentation project to produce at least one significant manual. For smaller documentation projects, the work in a task is greatly reduced.

One writer can perform all DDM tasks or he can delegate some activities to support services, such as word processing, graphic arts, and reproduction.

TASK 1 - PLAN
DOCUMENTATION
PROJECT

This task covers overall planning for the documentation project.

When you plan the project, you analyze the project objectives, scope, and audiences to determine what document or documents are necessary. Then you describe those documents with a content statement. You also define overall format guidelines that apply to all documents on your document list. These guidelines include such things as basic page format and text and graphic approaches.

You also define development priorities, overall review requirements, general word processing and production requirements, and a development scenario for each type of document.

Two outputs of project planning focus the planning and development of all the documents in the project. The first is a project plan. The second is a project writing guide, which includes project-wide text and format considerations. For single document projects, these outputs are usually only a page or two. A management review of the project plan usually occurs for multi-document projects.

Tasks 2 through 10 of the DDM are performed for each document in the documentation project.

TASK 2 - PLAN DOCUMENT CONTENT

This task begins the development of a single document. You define requirements, outline the document content, and specify the development schedule and resources.

To define requirements, you use your content statement from the project plan as a starting point and determine the specific objectives, scope, purpose, and audience of the document. Once you have defined in detail the purpose and audience of the document, you structure the document and outline its organization and content.

Then you line up your support services, name your reviewers, set a development schedule, and identify distribution requirements. You may schedule a review to obtain agreement on the document requirements, since they are the foundation for your development efforts. Also, during this task, you develop production control forms. Finally, you set up a project file to maintain a development history and to provide information for later updates of the document.

The output of this task is the part of the document plan that specifies the text and development of the document. The size of the document plan is proportional to the size of the document being planned — usually between 10% and 25% of the size of the document.

TASK 3 - PLAN DOCUMENT FORMAT

In Task 1, Plan Documentation Project, you defined project-wide format guidelines. In this task, you adapt those guidelines to fit the specific document. You use the outline prepared in Task 2 to develop sample pages to confirm that the proposed document format works with the specified content.

The outputs of this task are page samples and descriptive notes explaining the format standards. These complete the document plan. As a result of this task, you expand on the information in the project writing guide.

The outputs of Tasks 2 and 3 together form the document plan.

TASK 4 - REVIEW DOCUMENT PLAN AND COMMIT TO WRITING

This task is a major review checkpoint. You use it to get agreement from your reviewers that the document plan is sufficient to support the remaining tasks. Reviewers should identify incomplete, inaccurate, or inappropriate elements in the plan which might create problems in later tasks and cause schedules to slip. You use review input to correct and update your plan so it can be used to guide development of your first draft.

After review of the document plan and approval for development, you initiate production control. This means keeping track of the development of the document to ensure that deadlines and development milestones are met.

TASK 5 - WRITE FIRST DRAFT	During first draft writing, you fill in the document outline, following the standards in the project writing guide and the formats you developed. You write the detail sections first, develop your graphic ideas, and start a figure control list. Then you write the introductory and overview sections. In this task, writing style is not a concern. Rather, you concentrate on providing content for every item in the outline.
	For long, difficult, or sensitive documents, you may request a preliminary technical review of each section or chapter as you complete it.
TASK 6 - DEVELOP GRAPHICS	As you write the first draft, you note what graphics would be appropriate and start a figure control list. In this task, you complete the figure control list and collect graphic source material. For the first draft, you provide the best graphics you can. These may be your sketches; screen, form, and report layouts; copies of actual screens, forms, and reports; or photographs. All graphics, in some form, should appear in the draft copy presented for technical review.
	The outputs of Tasks 5 and 6 together form the technical review copy of the document.
TASK 7 - REVIEW TECHNICAL DETAIL	This task is the second major review checkpoint. Technical reviewers confirm the technical accuracy and completeness of the information before you spend time polishing sentences, completing the graphics, and refining the format.
	The output of this task is an annotated technical review copy with all technical corrections marked. You use the review input to identify missing or inaccurate material and to focus your rewrite and continued development.
TASK 8 - REWRITE AND COMPLETE GRAPHICS	You rewrite the draft to incorporate the corrections from the technical review and to refine the writing style. You now concentrate on improving sentences and paragraphs to express the content in the best possible way for the audience. You confirm that the writing follows the format standards you set up in the project writing guide. During this task, graphics that were incomplete in the first draft are finished.
	Several review and rewrite activities may be necessary to complete the rewrite task. For example, you may schedule a user review, which may include a formal field test of the document, and an edit to ensure that the format standards have been followed and the material is grammatically correct. You may also involve technical reviewers to confirm that rewriting did not introduce inaccuracies.
	The output of this task is your final document. You do not leave the rewrite task until you are satisfied with the organization of all the material and the content of all text and illustrations.
TASK 9 - REVIEW FINAL DRAFT AND COMMIT TO PUBLICATION	This last review task confirms that the document is correct in content and format. During this review, you check that all artwork is in the right place, pages are in the correct order, and the tables of contents match headings and page numbers. Management approves the document for printing.
	Your output from this task is the reproduction copy that is approved, corrected, and ready for printing.
TASK 10 - COORDINATE PUBLICATION	In this final task, you prepare instructions for final reproduction, may review printer's proofs before printing, coordinate the assembly of the materials, and specify distribution. Additionally, you perform clean-up of your project file and complete update instructions.

Your output from this task is the distributed document and all the information required to coordinate updates to the document.

DDM PROCESSING FLOW

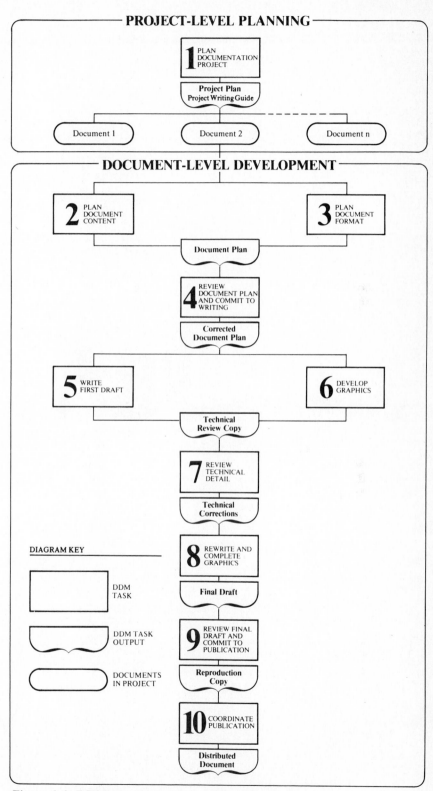

Figure 2.2 DDM processing flow with task outputs

Chapter 3

Using the DDM

Chapter 3

Using the DDM

To use the DDM effectively, you must plan and budget your time and resources. This chapter considers:
- Activities needed to meet task objectives.
- Support services for documentation development.
- Documentation project coordination.
- Integration of documentation development with your other work.

Activities to Complete Each DDM Task

The basic DDM tasks are the same regardless of the type of communication or the intended audience. These tasks provide the development structure.

To make the DDM work effectively, you must not skip any task. Tasks may be combined, however, and within each task you select only the activities required to complete the task. For example, if you do not know the subject matter, document planning must include information gathering. If the document is sensitive, you may want to schedule intermediate review steps. If you are writing a report against an established model, format planning involves looking over the model and adapting it to your requirements. You do not need activities for original format development.

As you analyze the needs of your document, you determine which activities it requires. Then when you have identified the activities needed to complete each task, you can plan and schedule your development effort.

The table in Figure 3.1 shows a master list of activities to consider for each DDM task and refers to chapters where you can find discussions of the skills needed to perform each activity. Many of the activities, such as review or production coordination, require similar skills. Therefore, the arrangement of the remaining parts of this book is *by function,* not by DDM task.

Each time an activity says "Write" or "Incorporate changes," it is assumed that you submit the material for some form of word processing. When an activity says "Make copies," it assumes you use reproduction services appropriate to produce the quantity and quality needed at that time.

TASK AND OBJECTIVES	ACTIVITIES TO CONSIDER	CHAPTER
1 - PLAN DOCUMENTATION PROJECT Initiate the documentation project, determine the work to be done, and define development requirements.	☐ Gather information. ☐ Define project scope and objective. ☐ Define audiences. ☐ Develop document list. ☐ Determine presentation media. ☐ Determine overall format guidelines for each medium. ☐ Define document priorities. ☐ Specify activities to complete DDM tasks. ☐ Define development scenario. ☐ Define field test structure. ☐ Write project design section of the project plan. ☐ Write the development requirements section. ☐ Begin project writing guide. ☐ Hold management review of project plan.	4 4 4 4 2, 4 4, 11 4 3, 4 4 7 4 4 4, 12 6
2 - PLAN DOCUMENT CONTENT Define the requirements for a document, outline its content, and specify the schedule and resources.	☐ Review the project plan. ☐ Define the document scope and purpose. ☐ Develop a detailed profile of the audience. ☐ Write the requirements statement section of the document plan. ☐ Hold management and user reviews of the requirements statement. ☐ Gather content information. ☐ Prepare the topic outline. ☐ Hold technical review of topic outline. ☐ Prepare an extended outline. ☐ Plan case study. ☐ Name reviewers. ☐ Specify support services needed. ☐ Prepare the development schedule. ☐ Define distribution requirements. ☐ Estimate number of copies needed. ☐ Write the schedule and resources section of the document plan. ☐ Prepare a development control form, a figure control list, and any other necessary production control forms. ☐ Set up project file.	5 5 5 5 6 5 5 6 5 5, 12 5 5, 14 5 5, 16 5 5 5, 14 3
3 - PLAN DOCUMENT FORMAT Adapt overall project format guidelines to the document and develop prototype pages.	☐ Review overall format guidelines. ☐ Establish illustration standards for figures. ☐ Develop page formats. ☐ Prepare sample pages with descriptive notes. ☐ Develop typing instructions. ☐ Maintain project file and project writing guide.	4, 5, 11 12 5, 11 5 5, 14 3, 12

Figure 3.1 Master list of activities for each DDM task (part 1 of 3)

TASK AND OBJECTIVES	ACTIVITIES TO CONSIDER	CHAPTER
4 - REVIEW DOCUMENT PLAN AND COMMIT TO WRITING Confirm that the plan is sufficient to guide the remaining tasks.	☐ Assemble the document plan. ☐ Write cover memo. ☐ Distribute to reviewers. ☐ Hold review meeting. ☐ Incorporate review changes. ☐ Obtain management approval to begin writing.	5 6 6 6 6 6
5 - WRITE FIRST DRAFT Flesh out the outline with words and identify what illustrations are necessary.	☐ Review the document plan. ☐ Review the project writing guide. ☐ Brief the typist. ☐ Write the detail sections. ☐ Write the introductions to the detail sections. ☐ Write the chapter overviews. ☐ Write the chapter summaries. ☐ Write the preface. ☐ Write the introduction to the document. ☐ Write the reader's comment form. ☐ Prepare the figure control list. ☐ Maintain production control, project writing guide, and project file.	8 8 14 8 8 8 8 8 8 8 8, 14 3, 12, 14
6 - DEVELOP GRAPHICS Provide drafts of all figures and illustrations.	☐ Review figure control list. ☐ Gather the figures, such as forms, screens, reports, charts, graphs. ☐ Specify artwork to be done. ☐ Enter artwork requirements on the figure control list. ☐ Sketch other illustrations and turn over to graphic arts. ☐ Order binders, tabs, and paper. ☐ Maintain production control.	8, 14 13 13, 14 14 13, 14 14 14
7 - REVIEW TECHNICAL DETAIL Confirm the draft is technically accurate and complete.	☐ Assemble first draft with rough graphics. ☐ Write cover memo. ☐ Make copies. ☐ Distribute to technical reviewers. ☐ Hold review meeting.	6, 8 6 15 6 6
8 - REWRITE AND COMPLETE GRAPHICS Finish the document by incorporating review comments, refining the text, and completing the graphics.	☐ Incorporate changes from the technical review. ☐ Perform a personal review to identify problems. ☐ Incorporate changes. ☐ Prepare reference aids except index. ☐ Complete the graphics. ☐ Assemble rewritten draft and final graphics into a user review copy.	6, 9 9 9 10 13 6

Figure 3.1 Master list of activities for each DDM task (part 2 of 3)

TASK AND OBJECTIVES	ACTIVITIES TO CONSIDER	CHAPTER
	☐ Write cover memo.	6
	☐ Make copies.	15
	☐ Distribute to reviewers.	6
	☐ Hold review meeting.	6
	☐ Incorporate review changes.	6
	☐ Assemble field test version.	7
	☐ Make copies.	15
	☐ Prepare for the field test.	7
	☐ Hold pre-field test meeting.	7
	☐ Conduct field test.	7
	☐ Hold post-field test meeting.	7
	☐ Incorporate changes from the field test.	9
	☐ Prepare index.	10
	☐ Maintain production control, project writing guide, and project file.	3, 12, 14
9 - REVIEW FINAL DRAFT AND COMMIT TO PUBLICATION Confirm that the document is correct and has the intended format.	☐ Assemble the reproduction copy of the document.	10, 14
	☐ Check for figure placement, order of pages, accuracy of tables of contents; spot-check the index.	6
	☐ Write sign-off memo.	6
	☐ Deliver to management for sign-off review.	6
	☐ Incorporate any changes from sign-off review.	9
10 - COORDINATE PUBLICATION Oversee printing, assembling, and distributing of the document.	☐ Make copies.	15
	☐ Assemble document prototype.	15
	☐ Check reproduction.	15
	☐ Supervise assembly of the document.	15
	☐ Prepare distribution list.	16
	☐ Write distribution memo.	16
	☐ Direct document distribution.	16
	☐ Build historical and update files.	16
	☐ Provide additional updating information.	16
	☐ Set up a master correction copy.	16

Figure 3.1 Master list of activities for each DDM task (part 3 of 3)

TAILORING THE ACTIVITY LIST   Each document should have its own activity list. Usually when you tailor the activity list, you combine some activities and delete others that do not apply to your document. For example, a short report may have only a single illustration and may adapt a company-established report page format. It may have a single reviewer, who reads over the material and discusses it with you while you wait.

You can also be more specific about who performs an activity or how it is done, especially in the area of graphic arts and reproduction. For limited projects, you may even combine DDM tasks.

Development of a single document, such as a brochure, might combine the project and document planning tasks.

The special nature of your project may require that you add activities — extra reviews, for instance, or coordination of typesetting activities if your material is going to be typeset. Also, if you are going to coordinate a team of writers, you have to schedule meetings to review progress and keep everyone's work synchronized.

The activity list shown in Figure 3.2 was developed to produce a reference summary card as part of a larger documentation project. It eliminates many of the activities given in the master activity list. It also adds a few activities to take care of special production for the card. An asterisk (*) designates the added activities.

DDM ACTIVITY LIST FOR A REFERENCE SUMMARY CARD

1 - PLAN DOCUMENTATION PROJECT

Done at project initiation and not for each separate document in the project.

2 - PLAN DOCUMENT CONTENT

- ☐ Review the project plan and user's guide.
- ☐ Define reference card scope and purpose.
- ☐ Identify reviewers.
- ☐ Specify and schedule support services.
- ☐ Prepare the development timetable.
- ☐ Estimate number of copies needed.
- ☐ Prepare development control form.
- ☐ Define distribution requirements.
- ☐ Write the document plan.
- ☐ Set up project file.

3 - PLAN DOCUMENT FORMAT

- ☐ Review overall format guidelines.
- ☐ Develop card format.
- * ☐ Indicate placement of topics in the reference card.
- ☐ Develop typing instructions.
- ☐ Maintain project file and project writing guide.

4 - REVIEW DOCUMENT PLAN AND COMMIT TO WRITING

- ☐ Assemble requirements statement and card layout.
- ☐ Hold review meeting.
- ☐ Incorporate review changes.

5 - WRITE FIRST DRAFT

- ☐ Review the document plan.
- ☐ Review the project writing guide.
- ☐ Brief typist.
- ☐ Write the card text.
- ☐ Maintain production control, project writing guide, and project file.

Figure 3.2 Tailoring the activity list (part 1 of 2)

℗ of Sandra Pakin & Associates, Inc.

REFERENCE SUMMARY CARD ACTIVITIES (continued)

6 - DEVELOP GRAPHICS

☐ Gather the figures.
☐ Specify artwork to be done, and turn over to graphic arts.
☐ Order paper.

7 - REVIEW TECHNICAL DETAIL

☐ Assemble a prototype card with rough graphics and make copies.
☐ Meet with technical reviewers.

8 - REWRITE AND COMPLETE GRAPHICS

☐ Incorporate changes from the technical review.
☐ Perform a personal review to identify problems.
☐ Incorporate changes.
* ☐ Send to graphic arts for typesetting and production preparation.
* ☐ Check work from graphics.
* ☐ Make copies of work from graphics and assemble for review.
☐ Meet with user reviewers.
☐ Incorporate review changes.
* ☐ Submit for graphic corrections.
☐ Maintain document control, project writing guide, and project file.

9 - REVIEW FINAL DRAFT AND COMMIT TO PUBLICATION

☐ Re-check final reference card.
☐ Write sign-off memo.
☐ Deliver to management for sign-off review.
☐ Incorporate any changes from sign-off review.

10 - COORDINATE PUBLICATION

☐ Prepare printing and folding instructions and deliver to print shop.
☐ Direct document distribution.
☐ File artwork for future updates.

Figure 3.2 Tailoring the activity list (part 2 of 2)

Support Services for Documentation Development

Although a writer can do all the typing, graphic development, and copying associated with the document development, it is more cost-effective to use various support personnel for:

- Word processing
- Graphic arts
- Assembly of drafts
- Reproduction
- Purchasing

Word Processing. This is the primary development support. Most of the DDM tasks require some form of typed output — from plans to actual text. Additionally, the DDM specifies at least one rewrite of the text draft. As a result, using word processing equipment instead of typewriters can save considerable effort. However, this book uses the term *word processing* to mean the typed preparation of a draft — whether it is prepared on a typewriter or on a word processing system. The term *typist* identifies the person who uses the word processing equipment, regardless of that person's job title.

Graphic arts. Figures and illustrations support the written text. Having someone other than the writer prepare them saves the writer time. Often a secretary or administrative assistant is available to help with the basic graphic work, or your company may have a graphic arts or advertising department whose services you can use.

This book uses the term *graphic arts* (performed by a *graphic artist*) to mean any service that prepares figures and illustrations. If your secretary does this preparation, he is acting as the graphic artist.

Assembly of drafts. This involves pasting down the figures, marking pages for reproduction, and putting the copies together. Typically a secretary, administrative assistant, or the word processing unit assembles the drafts. Occasionally, for special documents, such as reference cards or brochures, a graphic artist prepares the final copy for reproduction.

Reproduction. This books uses the term *reproduction* or *reproduction services* to cover any means of duplicating the document, such as an office copier or offset printing press.

You need copies of the DDM outputs for review and revision and copies of the final draft for distribution. Whoever ordinarily does the copying can use the office copier to make review copies. The company print shop usually prints the field test draft, if several copies are needed, and the final materials. Or you can send them to some other reproduction service for printing.

Purchasing. This books uses the term *purchasing* for the person or unit responsible for ordering such supplies as binders, tabs, and paper.

The DDM does not require that any of these support services be available as separate entities or departments. Anyone with the requisite knowledge can do the necessary functions.

Project Coordination

Every documentation project requires coordination — guiding the material through writing, review, and production. Coordination of the documentation project includes:

- Project reporting.
- Maintaining the project writing guide.
- Maintaining the project file.

PROJECT REPORTING

There are two types of project reporting:
- Interim progress reports to management
- Development time records

Reports to Managment

Management should receive regular reports on the documentation project status. The more critical the deadlines, the more often you should make these reports. Your report should include the following topics:

- Progress since the last report. A summary development control form conveys this information graphically and in the least amount of space.
- Plans. Work scheduled for completion before the next progress report.
- Problems. Anything that affects the documentation development or schedule. For example, if design of a particular application feature is behind schedule, this may also delay the documentation. Whenever possible, suggest solutions to the problems.

Time Records

Estimates of the time required to develop a document vary with:

- Type of document
- Complexity of the material
- Experience and skill of the writer
- Reviewer and support service needs

Maintaining records of the time spent in each task provides historical information for estimating the development time of other documents.

MAINTAINING THE PROJECT WRITING GUIDE

The project writing guide contains the text and graphics format standards for both the project and individual documents within the project. As the repository of all the format decisions for the project, it is useful to you as you write and to other writers working on the project or joining the project later. It serves as a guideline to the editor, who checks that format standards have been followed, and aids the writer responsible for updating the material.

The project writing guide may be an adaptation of existing company standards or instructions created specifically for the project. To maintain project-wide compatability, you amend the writing guide to reflect changes to the format standards as the project progresses.

The project writing guide for this book appears in Appendix B.

MAINTAINING THE DOCUMENTATION PROJECT FILE

Preparation for update begins when development begins. During development, you collect information to support update and keep it in the project file. Later, you cull the data to form the document update file.

The project file provides a history of the documentation effort. The file for the project should contain the project plan and project status reports. During document development, you should also include the following in the project file:

- Memos and pertinent correspondence, especially when they detail some significant change in concept, content, or scope.
- All pertinent source material.
- Various drafts with reviewers' comments.
- A complete, unmarked copy of the current draft to use as the correction master.
- A personnel checklist, listing all technical and administrative personnel who worked on the project and their contribution and responsibilities.
- Project writing guide.

™ of Sandra Pakin & Associates, Inc.

Integrating Documentation Development with Other Work

Any structured development methodology can easily incorporate the DDM. Integrating the DDM tasks with your other development work eliminates duplication of planning and information-gathering efforts and better ensures that documentation is ready when needed.

INTEGRATING
DOCUMENTATION
WITH SYSTEM LIFE
CYCLE

To produce system user documentation, you can integrate DDM documentation development tasks into the system development cycle. Most system development methodologies have one or more phases for the following:

- Requirements Definition
- General Design
- Business System or External Design
- Computer System or Internal Design
- Program Design
- Programming
- Testing
- Installation

You can integrate the DDM tasks with these phases or those of a similar system development methodology as follows.

After approval of the General Design, you know the scope of the development project. You can initiate the documentation project and do:

Task 1 - Plan Documentation Project

Prior to document planning, the externals of the system or application must be defined and the screen and report layouts prepared. Therefore, work on individual documents should not begin until approval of the Business System or External Design. The system documentation that you produce in the early development phases provides enough information for you to prepare the document plan and begin writing the first draft.

Thus, when the Business System Design is complete, you can do:

Task 2 - Plan Document Content
Task 3 - Plan Document Format
Task 4 - Review Document Plan and Commit to Writing

Also, you can begin:

Task 5 - Write First Draft
Task 6 - Develop Graphics

If the business design is not frozen when you begin writing, be prepared for changes, delays, and extra effort in the documentation.

By working on the first draft concurrently with Internal Design, Program Design, and Programming, you can easily incorporate system changes into the documentation. Your documentation goal is to have a draft available for technical review when programming is complete. When the draft is complete, do:

Task 7 - Review Technical Detail

The technical review may, in fact, be part of the system test. Then you can rewrite and prepare a field test draft. In time for on-site testing, do:

Task 8 - Rewrite and Complete Graphics

If the document field test is complete at the end of on-site testing, you can prepare the final draft and publish the document. So while the system is being installed, you do:

Task 9 - Review Final Draft and Commit to Publication
Task 10 - Coordinate Publication

By integrating documentation development with your system development, you have documentation available for on-site testing. And tested documentation is ready for distribution when the system is turned over to a production status.

INTEGRATING
DOCUMENTATION
WITH A STUDY

Most studies, such as a survey of new equipment or the development of a long-range strategy, end with the presentation of a formal report. If you determine documentation requirements early in the study, you can integrate documentation development with the study.

Consider, for example, an assignment to make an equipment selection. The study ends with a formal purchase recommendation — a report to write. Too often a report of this type is not even planned until all the study work is complete. Then it is difficult to assemble the report data and find missing information. Integrating the documentation tasks with the study simplifies the writing of the report because you can organize information when it is available and eliminate the last minute rush to plan, structure, and write your report.

Figure 3.3 shows the integration of DDM tasks with study tasks.

STUDY TASKS	DDM TASKS
1. Inititate study. 2. Plan the study — scope, information requirements, study method, resources. 3. Gather information.	Task 1 - Plan Documentation Project Task 2 - Plan Document Content Task 3 - Plan Document Format Task 4 - Review Document Plan and Commit to Writing
4. Analyze data and reach conclusions.	Task 5 - Write First Draft Task 6 - Prepare Graphics Task 7 - Review Technical Detail
5. Present tentative conclusions and recommendations.	Task 8 - Rewrite and Complete Graphics Task 9 - Review Final Draft and Commit to Publication Task 10 - Coordinate Publication
6. Present report.	

Figure 3.3 Integration of DDM tasks with a study

In Conclusion

The number and kind of activities required to complete a DDM task vary with the complexity and scope of the documentation project and the specific document. Part of the planning task involves determining which activities you need.

Regardless of the scope of the documentation, you skip no DDM task. You may combine some tasks, or you may find that a task requires only a few activities and little time to complete. You may delegate some of the activities to others. The objectives are to follow the DDM sequence, tailor it to your needs, and integrate it with your other work.

Part 2

PLANNING

Just as requirements definition and design precede programming, planning precedes writing for every documentation assignment.

A well-planned project is your best assurance of producing documentation that meets project goals and is developed on schedule. Planning skills are needed to perform the first three DDM tasks:

- Task 1 - Plan Documentation Project
- Task 2 - Plan Document Content
- Task 3 - Plan Document Format

The first task is project-wide planning. The second and third planning tasks are performed for each document in the project plan.

Chapters 4 and 5 discuss the planning activities needed to complete these tasks.

Chapter 4 - Project Planning

In project planning, you prepare the overall design for the documentation project. This involves identifying the number and type of documents required, the audiences to be reached, and the types of reviews and reviewers; standardizing the approach to development and production; and formulating development requirements. This chapter discusses each of these project planning topics.

Chapter 5 - Document Planning

Document planning is the detailed specification of a single document. This chapter covers all aspects of document planning, including specifying the document requirements, content outline, page format, schedule, and resources.

Chapter 4

Project Planning

Chapter 4
Project Planning

You perform project planning *once* for each documentation project. In project planning, you analyze the project objectives, scope, and audiences to determine needed documents, overall format guidelines, and development requirements. You state your decisions in a project plan for management approval, and you begin a project writing guide of text and graphic standards.

You need to plan the project whether you are producing a single document or a set of documents. Depending on the size of the project, preparation of a project plan takes from a day or two to a few weeks. Less work and time are involved when you are producing a single document, and even less if the document is short.

This chapter discusses the steps you perform during project planning:
- Analyzing needs.
- Identifying documents.
- Establishing overall format guidelines.
- Determining development requirements.

It concludes with a checklist of the contents of a project plan.

Needs Analysis

The project you are working on inherently defines the need for documentation. You may first express this need in a general problem statement:
- We need help screens.
- We need a long-range strategy report.
- We need a newsletter to keep people in the department informed of what we are doing and to inform our customers too.
- We have to market, install, and support our application package.

The general problem statement may suggest whether you are planning a single- or multiple-document project. You test assumptions during project planning. You must:
- State the project's objectives for the documentation.
- Define functions covered by the documents.
- List the various audiences for the documentation and specify their information needs.

Only then are you ready to build the document list — to say what documents are necessary and what their make-up should be.

For example, the statement "We need a long-range strategy report" suggests a single document. But once you have defined audiences, it may turn out that you need three documents: an executive summary for top management, a concepts and conclusions report for other management, and a detailed report for the implementers of the strategy. Or the dynamics of the strategy project may suggest producing both a preliminary and a final report.

STATING OBJECTIVES

You determine your documentation objectives by answering some basic questions. What are you trying to achieve through the documentation? What problem or situation is stimulating the need for documentation? The following problems are typical:

- Support the installation of distributed processing systems in our warehouses.
- Reduce calls to the service desk for common problems.
- Address exceptions raised in the last EDP audit review.
- Provide help screens with the new online application.
- Customize the vendor documentation for the new software we purchased and modified.
- Raise morale in the department and keep everyone informed about what is going on.

Once you determine the objectives, you can plan how to meet them.

DEFINING FUNCTIONS

Next, you need to analyze the problem and determine what functions need documenting. Installing systems in a distributed environment, for instance, means considering all aspects of running and using the system — computer operations, administrative controls, interfaces with headquarters, applications, management reporting, application development, and so forth. Documentation may be needed in all these areas.

The objective of reducing calls to the service desk for common problems initially suggests the need for a troubleshooting guide. But perhaps the problem goes deeper — perhaps the user or operator does not have appropriate reference materials. Your analysis may uncover the need for reference cards, a case study, or a newsletter. In this case, documentation may not solve the entire problem. Perhaps the user did not receive the proper training or needs training follow-up. Perhaps you need a regular meeting of users. Because these other needs may affect your documentation requirements, you should consider them in the project plan.

IDENTIFYING AUDIENCES

Identifying reader groups or audiences means stating who is going to read and act on the documentation you produce. It is a necessary step in determining kinds of documents needed and in developing an appropriate approach and structure for the documentation.

List as many audiences of the documentation as you can think of. As you analyze your audience list and as the project progresses, you may add or eliminate audiences.

For example, the audiences for a long-range strategy report may be MIS management, the DP steering committee, and other management affected by the strategy. But there may be secondary audiences, such as departmental people whose jobs the report affects. These secondary audiences may need specific information, even though they are not on the report distribution list.

There are many audiences for user operations documentation. Data entry operators enter, validate, and correct data, and perhaps distribute reports. A supervisor or lead operator performs control functions and maintains the equipment. Management uses the reports to make business decisions. Other users may have responsibility for preparing different inputs and balancing or confirming control reports.

Document Identification

In determining documentation requirements, you build a document list based on the information in your needs analysis. Then for each document, you specify the presentation medium, name the primary audience, and write a content statement.

BUILDING THE DOCUMENT LIST

Use the project's documentation objectives, the identified functions, and audience analysis to produce the document list. Consider each type of document, including manuals, reference cards, brochures, summary sheets, and so forth. Ideally:
- Readers should get only the information they need.
- Large blocks of text should not be repeated in several documents.

The document list may evolve by function or by audience. For example, titles like "Data Entry Operator's Guide," "Salesman's Instructions," and "Manager's Overview" suggest documents defined by audience, whereas "Order Taking and Billing," "Management Reports," and "How to Use the 674 Terminal" suggest documents defined by function.

Documents defined by audience are useful when audience responsibilities do not overlap. Each audience, then, gets only the information it needs. Marketing brochures, for instance, vary in detail as the audience changes from user management to technical management to technical staff.

Documents defined by function are useful when you cannot predict the exact audience or when all audiences require the information. A single document on using a terminal, for example, can be written if all audiences — programmers, data entry operators, and users — use the terminal.

REVIEWING THE DOCUMENT LIST

Review your document list for completeness and structure. If you covered all the information needs and if each document is unique (either by function or by audience), you have no further structuring to do. A sales accounting system may require a salesman's guide, a data entry operator's guide, an administrative office guide, and a billing explanation for customers. These four pieces make up the document list with none in the same category.

On the other hand, the documentation for a multi-function or distributed system may require more structuring. For example, a payroll system installed in a number of local offices has a pre-installation brochure, a user's guide, and a reference summary card for the local office user; a brochure for employees; and a financial office procedures manual for headquarters. These five documents are distributed among three audiences. Figure 4.1 shows this document list as a hierarchical chart.

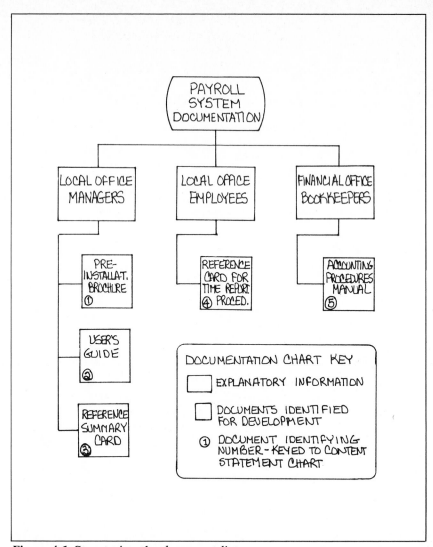

Figure 4.1 Structuring the document list

Visual structuring of the document list has value, particularly in larger documentation projects. You can easily see what documents you have and identify omissions or overlapping documents.

DETERMINING MEDIA — For each document in the document list, specify the presentation medium. For example, media to consider include system overview brochure, wall chart, reference card, tutorial, primer, detailed operator's guide. If you can estimate the approximate number of pages, do so. Determining the presentation medium for each document makes production planning easier.

NAMING THE PRIMARY AUDIENCE — The information needs of the primary audience affect such things as content, level of detail, and language. Be sure to specify the primary audience so content and style suit this audience's requirements.

WRITING A CONTENT STATEMENT — A content statement is a brief description of each document on the document list. The statement should include the purpose and intended audience of each document. This statement helps reviewers of your plan understand the rationale behind each document. Figure 4.2 shows the content statment for Figure 4.1.

NO.	DOCUMENT	DESCRIPTION	PRIMARY AUDIENCE	MEDIUM
1	Pre-installation Brochure	Short introduction on system's operational benefits and review of the installation schedule.	General and line managers	Fanfold
2	User's Guide	Explanation of procedures for operating system, including running and correcting reports and checking employee input.	Managers who approve time reports for employees	Manual— 3-ring binder
3	Reference Summary Card	Review of operational commands for running the system.	Managers who operate the system	One-page card
4	Reference Card for Time Reporting Procedures	Graphic review of the punching in and out procedures, plus time report verification.	All employees	Poster
5	Accounting Procedures Manual	Overview of accounting portion of the system and explanation of operational procedures.	Bookkeepers	Manual— 3-ring binder

Figure 4.2 Content statement for the document list

Overall Format Guidelines

During project planning, you establish format guidelines for the project as a whole so all related documents form a set. These guidelines cover basic format and writing and graphic standards. Each document's page format, developed during document planning (Chapter 5), adheres to these guidelines. Format guidelines constitute the project writing guide that you use and maintain throughout the project.

BASIC FORMAT   During project planning, you must determine:
- Types of bindings for the various media; for example, three-ring binders for manuals, staples for brochures.
- Page size; for example, 8-1/2″ by 11″ to go in a binder, to fit folded in a standard envelope, or to read clearly when posted on a wall.

- Margins and column width to accommodate the type of binding and page size to yield a readable document.
- Placement of required control information; such as page number, manual or document name, version date.
- Special paper; for example, logo paper for manuals or a special grease resistant or coated paper for reference cards used in the plant.

Some organizations have standards for the basic format. If yours does, you have little extra work to do. You simply review your organization's standards to be sure you understand what is required and what you can vary. If no standards exist or if your company standards need modification, you can receive help in making these decisions from the discussions in Chapter 11, "Page Format and Layout," and Chapter 12, "Format Standards."

WRITING AND GRAPHIC STANDARDS

Establishing rules for text and graphic formats that apply to all documents in the project takes place during project planning. These standards include:
- Style guidelines
- Text format
- Graphic approach

Style Guidelines

Acceptable variations in punctuation, capitalization, spelling, and writing style exist within standard English usage. A style guideline ensures consistency by specifying which of the variations are standard for the document, the project, or the organization. For example, one style guide recommends spelling out all numbers under 100; another recommends spelling out all numbers under ten. Neither is more right than the other.

If your company has established style guidelines, use them. If you do not know whether your company has guidelines, check with the publication or advertising department or other similar group.

If your company does not have established style guidelines, one of the standard texts, such as the *University of Chicago Manual of Style,* can serve the purpose. Additionally, select a dictionary as the authority for all spelling questions. It is also wise to select a data processing dictionary or glossary, such as the *IBM Data Processing Glossary,* for the spelling of data processing terms.

Text Format

Text format standards specify the way headings and text are typed, entered, or typeset. The text format standards determine typing instructions and guidelines for marking up the text for data entry or typesetting. Therefore, the guidelines should cover all the indenting, spacing, and type variations.

Graphic Approach

Two basic decisions on the use of graphics in the various documents should be made during project planning:
- Source of the graphic content
- Graphic style

Source of Graphic Content. If you intend to show illustrations such as reports, screens, and input forms with actual data, then early in the project, you must determine sources of the data. For example, to provide consistent data throughout one or a set of documents in the project plan, you might specify that a case study be developed.

Graphic Style. The style of graphics for documents should be consistent and suited to the project. Cartoon-style or stick figures, for example, may or may not be appropriate for all documents in the project. Style determinations should occur before graphic development begins. Also, you may want photographs, particularly for equipment documentation. In this case, an early decision helps the production planning and allows enough lead time to obtain and process the photographs.

Development Requirements

Development requirements are part of the overall project plan and consist of:
- Development priorities
- Review requirements
- Production requirements
- Development scenario

The project plan contains all the development requirements. They form the basis for both the schedule and resources specified for each individual during document planning.

DEVELOPMENT PRIORITIES

You must establish development priorities so you can schedule your writing time, the reviews, and production. To establish priorities, first consider external influences:
- Imposed delivery dates beyond your control. For example, a government agency requires a report by a specific date.
- System development schedules. What portions of the system will be ready for testing and when?

Then consider the documents themselves:
- If some documents assume information available in another document, the prerequisite document receives first consideration.
- Management summaries are always easier to write after the detailed documents are complete.
- Material for new or untrained audiences should have high priority, to reduce trouble calls and technical support requirements.

If the document list is simple, arrange the documents in order of importance or need. If the document list is a hierarchical chart, write a priority number next to the document name. If some of your priority decisions are controversial, include an explanation in the project plan supporting your decisions.

REVIEW REQUIREMENTS

Every project needs reviewers. Your organization, the sensitivity of the project, and the kinds of audiences help you define your review requirements.

Types of Reviewers

At minimum, each document requires four types of reviewers:
- Technical. To ensure that the technical content is accurate.
- Management. To ensure that the material reflects corporate image and policies and that management approves the allocation of resources for development.
- User. To ensure that the procedures suit the user's working environment and that the presentation is appropriate for the audience.
- Editorial. To ensure that the document adheres to all standards and that the language is grammatical, consistent, and easy to read.

Types of Review   The DDM specifies three review tasks:
- Task 4 - Review Document Plan and Commit to Writing. To confirm that the document's plan is complete and accurate enough to begin writing and graphic development.
- Task 7 - Review Technical Detail. To check the complete first draft to be sure the organization is workable and the technical detail is accurate enough to begin the rewrite function.
- Task 9 - Review Final Draft and Commit to Publication. To perform the final quality assurance review before publication to ensure the final draft and graphics read and look as expected and are complete enough for reproduction.

Additional review activities are planned within tasks depending on the needs of the project. These include:
- Project plan review. To ensure management and user agreement on the plans for the project as a whole, including number and type of documents and development scenario.
- Requirements statement and topic outline review. To clarify misunderstandings of purpose and content of a document and prevent wasted development time.
- Edit. To correct inconsistencies in terminology, format, and style while assuring that such standard items as spelling, grammar, and punctuation are also correct. Editing takes place after the draft has received all updates and technical corrections.

Other reviews that might be included, depending on the size and complexity of the project, are:
- Field test. Used to try out the document in a user environment. Field testing is the subject of Chapter 7.
- Chapter or section review. Used during first draft writing to ensure that the material covers the needed information properly and to catch such problems as illogical organization before you have written the entire draft.
- Graphic review. Used particularly for original illustrations, to avoid spending development time for graphics and illustrations that are inaccurate, too difficult, or misdirected.

Managing the   During project planning, you determine your project-wide review
Review Process   needs. They include the types of reviews and reviewers needed and the points where you should schedule reviews for each document type. For example, you can schedule reviews for each planning task or set up a comprehensive planning review (Task 4) when you have completed all planning.

Not every review involves all types of reviewers. For example, since plans are internal documents, editorial review is not needed to polish style. Also, editorial and user reviews may not be needed during the technical review of the first draft.

During project planning, you also determine how to manage review. You decide how reviewers will receive the material and how you will collect comments and resolve reviewer differences. Chapter 6 discusses managing the review process.

If any documents will be field tested, you must structure the field test. You must determine which documents to field test, how much time to allow per test, and how many and what kinds of people to involve. You must also decide who conducts the test, and how you get the results. Chapter 7 discusses field testing.

PRODUCTION REQUIREMENTS

As part of development requirements, you must determine what word processing, graphic arts, and printing resources are necessary and available. You must decide:

- How to prepare drafts — typed or prepared on a word processing system locally or by a central pool — and who will proofread each version.
- How to prepare final text — typed or typeset — and if typeset, who will do it.
- What printing method to use — copier or offset printing — and any preparation requirements for using the method.
- What project-wide graphic arts to use and what graphic support services are available.
- What procedure to follow in ordering supplies, such as binders, tabs, and special paper.

Also, find out from any support services you are using the lead times they need, typical turnaround times, and instructions for scheduling, submitting work, and requesting rush services.

Chapter 14 discusses how to work with support services, and Chapter 15 discusses production methods.

DEVELOPMENT SCENARIO

During project planning, you define a development scenario for each type of document to help you understand the scope of the work. In document planning, you use the development scenario to prepare a development schedule and production control forms for the specific document.

To define a development scenario, list the activities you need to complete each task. Tailor the master activity list in Figure 3.1, considering your review structure and production plans and the nature of the documents.

Then use the activity list to define development checkpoints as shown in Figures 4.3 and 4.4. A checkpoint occurs when the material changes hands — when it goes to review, to typing, to testing and when it returns to you for further development.

TO DEVELOP THE XYZ USER'S GUIDE

☐ Develop document plan (DDM Tasks 2 and 3).
☐ Review plan and revise (DDM Task 4).
☐ Write first draft and develop graphics (DDM Tasks 5 and 6).
☐ Type the first draft and assemble review copy.
☐ Review first draft for technical accuracy (DDM Task 7).
☐ Rewrite the draft and complete graphics (DDM Task 8).
☐ Type the rewrite.
☐ Conduct user review.
☐ Incorporate user comments.
☐ Type corrections and prepare the final draft.
☐ Review final draft (DDM Task 9).
☐ Make final corrections.
☐ Print the copies (DDM Task 10).
☐ Assemble the copies.

Figure 4.3 Development scenario for a user's guide

You can establish a checkpoint at any development milestone — at the end of a DDM task or set of tasks or at the end of an activity within a task. Figures 4.3 and 4.4 show the checkpoints developed for two sample project situations. For your information, the DDM tasks completed before each checkpoint are noted in parentheses. Task 1, Plan Documentation Project, is not included because this list is developed during Task 1.

In Figure 4.4, the development checkpoints for a small report correlate almost directly with DDM tasks. The report requires few interim checkpoints.

TO DEVELOP A SHORT REPORT

☐ Plan report (DDM Tasks 2 and 3).
☐ Review the plan (DDM Task 4).
☐ Write the first draft and develop graphics (DDM Tasks 5 and 6).
☐ Type the first draft.
☐ Review technical detail (DDM Task 7).
☐ Rewrite and complete graphics (DDM Task 8).
☐ Type the final draft.
☐ Review the final draft and write cover memo (DDM Task 9).
☐ Make the copies (DDM Task 10).

Figure 4.4 Development scenario for a short report

The tailored activities list is your guide to the work to be done. The development scenario indicates at what points in the development you will need reviewers and support services. It is used in document planning when you set up a development schedule and the production control forms for the individual document.

Checklist for Project Plan

The outputs of project planning are a project plan and a project writing guide. This section includes a checklist for the contents of the project plan. Chapter 12, "Format Standards," concludes with a checklist for the contents of the project writing guide.

The project plan and project writing guide for this book appear in Appendix A and Appendix B, respectively.

The project plan consists of:
• Project design section
• Development requirements section

PROJECT DESIGN SECTION
Include the following in the project design section:
☐ Name of the project and its objectives.
☐ List or hierarchy chart of documents.
☐ Statement for each document defining the primary audience, content, presentation medium, and approximate number of pages.

DEVELOPMENT REQUIREMENTS SECTION
The development requirements section consists of the document

priorities, development scenario, review requirements, and production requirements.

Document Priorities
- ☐ Rank the documents in the project in development priority order. If you know specific due dates, list these also.

Development Scenario
- ☐ List the development checkpoints.

Review Requirements
- ☐ For each review checkpoint in the development scenario, identify the type of reviewers needed.
- ☐ State how you will distribute review material and collect comments.
- ☐ State how long each review period should last.
- ☐ Define the field test structure:
  - Documents to be field tested.
  - Time allowed per test.
  - Minimum number and kinds of people involved in the field test.
  - People responsible for conducting the field test.
  - Procedure for getting the field test results.

See Part 3, "Review," for further information.

Production Requirements
- ☐ For each production checkpoint in the development scenario, state the production support resources needed.
- ☐ State how the drafts and final copy will be prepared.
- ☐ State the printing method to be used.
- ☐ State the special project-wide graphic arts needs and the support services available to accomplish them.

See Part 6, "Production," for further information.

Chapter 5
Document Planning

Chapter 5
Document Planning

In project planning, you prepare an overview plan for the entire project. Then when development begins on a specific document, such as a user's guide, a long-range strategy report, a feasibility study, or a brochure, you prepare a detailed plan for that document by:
- Defining requirements.
- Outlining the content.
- Developing the page format.
- Specifying the schedule and resources.

The result of this planning effort is the document plan.

Requirements Definition

For requirements definition, you determine the objectives, scope, purpose, and audience of the specific document. You write up this information in a requirements statement for the document. The requirements statement covers three areas of information to steer the development of the document:
- Subject overview
- Scope and purpose of the document
- Audience definition

SUBJECT OVERVIEW
The subject overview is a one- or two-paragraph statement of the subject prompting the documentation. For a user's guide, this section is the system overview and includes the purpose of the system, its general functions, and its processing flow from the point of view of the intended audience. For a long-range strategy report, this section is a mission statement. You write the subject overview to orient yourself and your reviewers to the subject of the document.

SCOPE AND PURPOSE
The document scope and purpose section amplifies the content information provided in the project plan. The document scope and purpose section answers the following questions:
- What is to be accomplished by the document?
- Why is it needed?
- How will it be used?
- What will it not do?
- How does it relate to other documents?
- Is a case study needed to provide consistent examples?

AUDIENCE DEFINITION
The audience definition section defines the experience level, expectations, and information needs of the intended audience. This is the

most critical section in the requirements statement.

Having a clear definition of the audience ensures that the document provides for maximum reader acceptance and functionality. For example, data entry operators need terminal and data entry instructions, but do not require discussions of the purpose and uses of management reports. Managers and general user groups do not need operator information or technical detail, but they expect overview discussions and conceptual explanations.

List Audiences Begin the audience definition by listing the various audiences from the project plan and identifying whether they are the primary or secondary audience. For example, an in-house newsletter for systems staff in various decentralized sites may have the following audiences:

- System coordinators – primary
- Programmers – primary
- Systems and operations management – secondary
- Secretarial and clerical personnel – secondary

In case of conflicts in level of detail, language use, approach, and so forth, you always settle in favor of the primary audience. If this resolution makes the material unintelligible to the secondary audience, you need to consider expanding the document list to include a document directed to that audience.

Profile Audience Groups Once you have identified the audiences, profile each audience group as thoroughly as possible:

- What type of work do they do?
- What are their interests and concerns?
- What are their skills and experience?
- What must they know about the subject of the document?
- What are the prerequisites for understanding this document?
- What do the readers expect to get out of the document? What should they know when they finish reading it?
- How interested in the subject are the readers? How will they react to the document? Are there any critical issues or potential controversies?

For example:

> *The system coordinator is in charge of the system. Among his responsibilities are starting up and shutting down the system each day, helping operators with troubleshooting and maintaining their service request log, ordering supplies, and attending the monthly coordinators' meeting.*
>
> *The coordinator is looking for two kinds of information:*
> - *How to perform specific coordinator procedures.*
> - *How to reduce the time he spends in day-to-day operator guidance.*
>
> *Most coordinators are operators who have been promoted to this supervisory position. They are fairly skilled in operations. However, this may be their first supervisory job. The manual should assume that coordinators and operators have had the vendor's training class on using the equipment. Its purpose is to provide specific company procedures for administrative tasks, such as ordering supplies.*

Outline Preparation

Preparing an outline forces you to write down and organize a set of topics about a subject. As you develop your outline, you can see whether you have the topics in a logical sequence compatible with the document's objectives. You can also determine what kinds of additional information you may need on the subject.

For short brochures and reference cards, the structure is closely tied to the format so you can define the content by an ordered list of topics.

For reports, product summaries, manuals, and other long or complicated documents, outline the content in two stages:

- Topic outline. A detailed listing of the major sections and subsections to provide an overview of the basic *organization* of the document. A visual table of contents (VTOC) may support the topic outline by showing the structure of the document or of document sections.
- Extended outline. A detailed outline or discussion of the *contents* of each section and subsection.

TOPIC OUTLINE   The topic outline structures the presentation of the material. The following guidelines should help you produce a reasonable topic outline:

- Use a model if you can.
- Select an organizing principle.
- Check your structure with a visual table of contents (VTOC).

Use a Model   To simplify your outlining task, use a model if one is available. Figure 5.1 shows a model outline that you could adapt to your document by including specific references at each applicable point.

Although models provide a starting point and can save planning effort, they are only guides and must be used carefully. They can rarely be used without modification. The user-oriented topics under "Processing" in the sample outline of Figure 5.1, for instance, may cover information not needed by an operator or management audience.

THE XYZ SYSTEM USER'S GUIDE

INTRODUCTION
A. Purpose of the system
B. Flow of information through the system
    1. System and user functions
    2. Inputs
    3. Processing the user needs to understand
    4. Outputs
C. System use
    1. Approvals to use
    2. What the system is suited for and not suited for
    3. Rules and standards in the use of the system
    4. Support for users of the system — supporting groups, education, manuals
D. Responsibilities

EQUIPMENT DESCRIPTION
For each piece of equipment, such as printer and display station:
A. Operating features and benefits
B. Operating instructions

Figure 5.1 Model outline for a user's guide (part 1 of 2)

℗ of Sandra Pakin & Associates, Inc.

THE XYZ SYSTEM USER'S GUIDE (continued)

INPUTS
A. What are they
B. Where do they come from and what must the user know or do before he is ready to prepare the input
C. Types of input transactions
D. Procedures for inquiry, online update or data entry transactions, requesting reports

PROCESSING
A. What does the system do to the inputs
B. How does the data base affect the use of the system
C. When should processing be done (schedules)
D. Working with operations (batch)
   1. Operating schedules
   2. Job submission — what is involved in submitting a job, what forms are required, how is a job packaged, how is a job delivered and received

OUTPUTS
A. Reports
   1. What kinds
   2. How are they read
   3. How are they checked
   4. How do they relate to the inputs or input transactions
   5. How are report statistics used
B. Files
   1. What kinds
   2. How are they related
   3. What control does the user have

SYSTEM AT WORK IN A SAMPLE ENVIRONMENT
How the user would use the system for a typical task, from planning to receipt of output

ERROR CORRECTION
A. Error messages
B. Correction procedures
C. Troubleshooting

REFERENCE AIDS
A. Glossary of terms
B. Index

Figure 5.1 Model outline for a user's guide (part 2 of 2)

Select an Organizing Principle

The organizing principle you choose for a document depends on the objectives of that document. Generally, the organization is most effective if you keep related information together. Your organizing principle works if it provides a reasonable organization for all your information. If you have a "miscellaneous" section or appendixes for information other than codes and error messages, re-evaluate your organizing principle.

The four main organizing principles used for documentation are:
- Logical
- Chronological
- Psychological
- Topical

Logical Organization. User's and data entry operator's guides are most typically organized logically, following the processing work flow. A system development guide outlines the necessary activities and tasks as they are performed, starting with project initiation and proceeding through all the tasks to installation.

Chronological Organization. Chronological organization is time-ordered. A computer operator's guide might be organized chronologically, tracking procedures performed during the day — from system start-up through system shut-down.

Psychological Organization. Psychological organization is results-ordered. It covers the most important topics first. The psychological organization provides a stronger presentation for a long-range strategy report, for instance, because it presents recommendations and conclusions first. Marketing materials stress benefits, and a psychological organization states these early.

Topical Organization. Sometimes the order of sections is not very important as long as all information on a topic is together. The organization is then topical, and you try to select topics that logically group information. A standards reference manual may be topically organized — for example, documentation standards, programming standards, testing standards, computer operations standards, and so forth. A newsletter, with regular columns on New Developments, Operator Tips, User Support, and Personality or Location Profiles, is arranged topically.

Check Your Structure   One of the most effective ways to check your document organization is a visual table of contents (VTOC). A VTOC shows the structure of your material. It helps you and your reviewers see the hierarchy of topics and shows the relationships between topics. The VTOC can define a general structure or organize specific topics. For example,

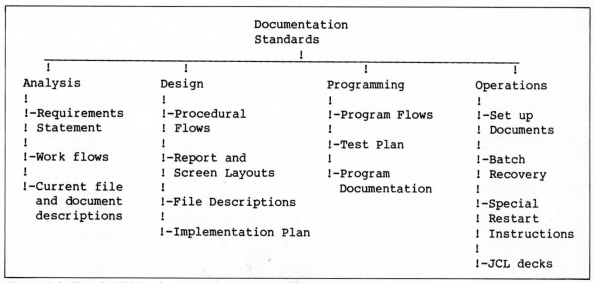

Figure 5.2 Typed VTOC of a manual section on documentation standards

Figure 5.2 shows how the documentation standards section of a standards manual may be organized around life cycle phases.

As you look over the VTOC you may identify topics that are not included or not placed properly. The VTOC above, for example, does not include standards for user documentation — and should. It also shows no topics for overall documentation considerations like maintaining the documentation and building a project file.

EXTENDED OUTLINE

The topic outline shows the major subjects of the document and its overall organization. The extended outline details the content before the lengthy writing process begins.

In the extended outline, you modify and expand topics to give a clearer picture of the content of each section. You indicate where illustrations from a case study are needed. You may also reorganize topics based on reviewers' comments and additional information gathering.

The extended outline may be a detailed content outline, a narrative description, or a combination of the two. For example, the following is a topic outline for the data base description section of the introduction to a manual:

1. *Financial System data base*
   a. *Organization*
   b. *Content*
   c. *Uses*
   d. *Benefits*

Outline Approach

The outline approach to an extended outline adds more specifics and expands on the information in the topic outline while maintaining the outline format:

1. *The Financial System data base*
   a. *Data base is organized to reflect the financial structure of the corporation and its reporting requirements. It includes:*
      (1) Corporate organization structure
      (2) Account data
      (3) Accounting structure
   b. *Data base includes actual operating data and budget data*
   c. *Data base is used to consolidate operating data totals throughout the corporation and to prepare monthly and year-end schedules and statements*
   d. *Major benefits include:*
      (1) Serves as a foundation for continuity and provides timely information
      (2) Serves as a collection point for historical data for analysis

Narrative Approach

The narrative approach to an extended outline expands on the information in the topic outline by describing the kind of discussion to be presented, for example:

1. *The Financial System as a data base application*
   This section tells how the data base is organized to reflect the financial structure of the corporation and its reporting requirements. The organization includes corporate organization structure, account data, and the accounting structure. It then explains that the data base includes actual operating data and budget data.
   It next discusses how the data base is used to consolidate

™ of Sandra Pakin & Associates, Inc.

operating data totals throughout the corporation to produce monthly schedules and statements. Finally, it points out that the data base approach provides data continuity, timely information, and historical data for analysis.

Comparison of the Two Approaches

Your goal is to write your outline in such a way that reviewers can evaluate the proposed content and scope of the material. Either approach can achieve this goal.

The outline approach exposes the structure of the individual paragraphs and provides a checklist for the eventual writing. The narrative approach talks about the content and creates an impression of the writing style of the completed manual. You may use either or both approaches depending on which conveys the matter and sense of the section most accurately to your reviewers.

Page Format for the Specific Document

During project planning, you developed the basic page format and the text and graphics standards and documented these in the project writing guide. For an individual document, you expand on the project's format guidelines:

*   Determine page format, which may be an adaptation of the project page format.
*   Prepare sample pages with descriptive notes.

ADAPTING THE PROJECT PAGE FORMAT

Most of the time, the project page format is suitable as is for a specific document in the plan. However, sometimes you have to adapt it for your document. For example, suppose one of several user's guides explains a set of reports, but the reports are too wide to fit on the width of an 8-1/2″ by 11″ page, even when reduced. This guide could accommodate those reports by adapting the format to allow

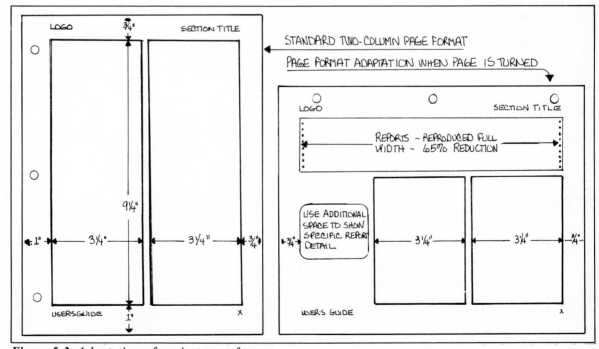

Figure 5.3 Adaptation of project page format

turning pages sideways. Continuity between this and other guides using the basic format is maintained by not changing text standards or the positioning of control information, as shown in Figure 5.3. Wherever possible, margin sizes are also maintained.

PREPARING
SAMPLE PAGES

Be sure to test your page format by preparing sample pages based on the outline information. These samples also provide reviewers with an example of how the final document will look.

Include some illustrations in your samples. For example, show how your document presents a screen or report description, and include some of the graphic devices you plan to use, such as callout numbers and shading.

Schedule and Resources

To publish and distribute the document, you need to specify:
- Support services requirements
- Reviewers
- Case study requirements
- Development schedule
- Number of copies needed
- Distribution requirements

This information builds on the information provided in the development requirements section of the project plan.

SUPPORT SERVICES
REQUIREMENTS

List specifically the support services you need:
- Word processing. Number of pages estimated for the first draft. Number of rewrite passes. This is the number of reviews you have scheduled for the material, plus rewrites from your personal review of the material.
- Graphic arts. What kinds of graphic art support do you anticipate? For example, drawing flow diagrams, preparing a title page, equipment photographs, typesetting, laying out pages of a reference card or brochure.
- Reproduction services. How will review drafts be copied? How will the final draft be copied? Are there special reproduction requirements, such as two-sided printing, spiral binding, special folding?
- Purchasing. What supplies must be ordered, such as binders, tabs, and pre-printed paper?

While you are determining the kind and amount of support services your development requires, determine the workload and estimated turnaround for each. You will need this information to specify your development schedule. Chapter 14, "Production Control," discusses how to work with these support services.

REVIEWERS

List the reviewers and identify at what point in the development they receive the document. Determine the time availability of all reviewers to schedule reviews. If the material is going to be field tested, define the specific field test structure in this section. Field testing is discussed in Chapter 7.

CASE STUDY
REQUIREMENTS

The case study provides consistent examples in the document and demonstrates selected system features. During document planning, you should define the scope of the case study and arrange for its development.

Scope has two dimensions: extent and content. *Extent* is that portion of the system demonstrated by the case study. Focusing on each audience's processing needs and the purpose of the document helps you determine the extent of the case study. A case study developed for operator training, for example, might concentrate on entry techniques and error correction. It would not require extensive report examples, essential in a case study developed to provide examples for a management user's guide.

Content refers to the specific system features and exceptions that the case study is to demonstrate. The case study should include the features and exceptions most frequently encountered or misunderstood in the processing environment of the audience. The case study may also include features and exceptions in the system that require special demonstration.

The case study should be developed in time for the technical review of the document, so reviewers can comment on the examples as well as the document text.

DEVELOPMENT SCHEDULE

The development schedule tracks development of the document beginning with first draft writing and ending with distribution of the completed document.

Build the development schedule using the development scenario defined during project planning. The development schedule specifies dates for the completion of each development checkpoint.

To develop a realistic schedule:

1. Determine the amount of time it will take you to develop the material.
2. Determine the elapsed time it will take to publish the material.
3. Use the information from 1 and 2 to build the schedule.

Determining Development Time

To determine development time, you must first estimate the number of pages in the final document. Document requirements may pre-establish the number of pages — for example, a six-page newsletter or an eight-to-twelve page brochure. Otherwise, the number of pages depends on how much information you have to convey.

After you have completed the outline, you should be able to predict the number of pages it will take to develop the content from the outline. Go through a copy of the outline and pencil in your estimate of the number of pages in each section. Add these up, and you have the estimated number of pages.

The amount of time a person devotes to developing a well-written document varies with his experience and skill and the complexity of the material. That is why it is important for you to keep a personal history of the time it takes you to develop material in hours per page. The more historical information you have on development timing, the better you can estimate your writing time for a new document.

This book uses three hours per page as a reasonable estimate to develop user documentation after the document plan is complete. Depending on the complexity and size of the document, planning might take up to an additional hour per page.

Multiply the estimated number of pages by the development hours per page. The result is the estimated development time. For example, a 100-page user's guide would take 300 hours, at three hours per page.

Determining the
Elapsed Time

Elapsed time is the number of weeks the development requires. It is affected by many factors, such as support service turnaround and the percentage of time commitment of writers and reviewers. For example, a writing job of 40 hours would take four weeks to complete if the writer was devoting only 25% of his time to the project.

To determine your elapsed time, divide the development time by the number of hours per day you will devote to documentation. For example, if you can work five hours a day on a 300-hour project, it will take 60 days or 13 weeks to complete the document.

Then find out word processing, graphic arts, and printing turnaround times for the amount of material you estimate. When you discuss this with word processing and graphic arts, get estimates for original work and corrections.

Finally, decide how much time to allow for each review and for the field test if you are going to conduct one.

Add up the times. Figure 5.4 shows an example. It assumes that typing and graphic arts preparation are done concurrently.

| CHECKPOINT | ELAPSED | |
	DAYS	WEEKS
First draft writing*	35	7.0
First draft typing	10	2.0
Technical review	5	1.0
Rewriting*	20	4.0
Typing the rewrite	8	1.5
User review	10	2.0
Final writing*	5	1.0
Final review	2	.5
Final corrections	2	.5
Printing	10	2.0
Assemble copies	2	.5
	109	22.0

*Includes production coordination activities, which account for about 15% of the writer's development work.

Figure 5.4 Estimating elapsed development time

Now you can predict the distribution date of the material by counting forward on a calendar the specified number of weeks.

If you discover that your target date is unacceptable, you can look for ways to adjust the elapsed time. You can overlap first draft writing with typing by submitting sections as you complete them. Then, you can reduce time allowed for review. Next, you can bring in temporary help for typing and send the material out for reproduction. Finally, depending on how much time you have allocated per week for writing, you might be able to reduce elapsed writing time by working longer per day or by adding additional writers.

If the revised distribution date of the material is still not acceptable, you might be able to distribute the user review copy as an interim version until you can complete the material.

Building the
Development Schedule

Knowing the elapsed times for various functions, you can also build the development schedule. Figure 5.5 shows an example based on the development scenario shown in Figure 4.3 and the elapsed times of Figure 5.4.

CHECKPOINT	DAYS	COMPLETE DATE
Write first draft and develop graphics.........	35	Feb. 19
Type the first draft; assemble review copy....	10	Mar. 5
Review the draft for technical accuracy......	5	Mar. 12
Rewrite the draft and complete graphics.....	20	Apr. 9
Type the rewrite.........................	5	Apr. 16
Conduct user reviews.....................	10	Apr. 30
Incorporate user comments...............	5	May 7
Type the corrections; prepare final draft.....	3	May 12
Review final draft........................	2	May 14
Make final corrections....................	2	May 18
Print the copies.........................	10	June 1
Assemble the copies......................	2	June 3

Figure 5.5 Specifying a development schedule. The schedule assumes that writing began on January 4 and that no development work is done on weekends.

Once you know the development schedule, you can prepare the production control forms for tracking the development of the document. Chapter 14, "Production Control," explains how to design these forms.

NUMBER OF
COPIES NEEDED

An early decision on the number of copies needed facilitates ordering supplies. Also, the number of copies to be published affects publication time estimates. The number can also affect distribution.

To determine the number of copies, start with the total number of copies required for the initial distribution. To this base number, add the number of copies required for:
- Filing and library back-up
- Complimentary copies
- Reasonable inventory

To determine the inventory number, consider the life of the document (one time, one year before revisions) and the new audience potential (new employees, new users).

DISTRIBUTION
REQUIREMENTS

During document planning, you can determine methods for distributing the material. Some possible distribution methods are:
- Deliver a complete document to each person on the distribution list individually.
- Drop-ship assembled materials to sites or departments for distribution by a local coordinator.
- Drop-ship unassembled materials — text, binders, tabs — to sites or departments for assembling and distribution by a local coordinator. This method is useful for a manual tailored for each user.

You can also decide whether you want each document numbered as a distribution control. Then your distribution list will show the specific copy given to each person on the list.

Checklist for the Document Plan

The output of Task 2, Plan Document Content, and Task 3, Plan Document Format, is the document plan. This section provides a checklist for the contents of each section of the document plan. With completion and approval of the document plan, you are ready to write the document. At this time, you also begin tracking production.

The document plan consists of:
- Requirements statement
- Outline
- Page format
- Schedule and resources

Additionally, you should update the project writing guide with information learned during document planning.

Include the following items in the document plan.

REQUIREMENTS STATEMENT
- ☐ Topic overview
- ☐ Scope and purpose of the document
- ☐ Detailed audience profile

OUTLINE
- ☐ Topic outline with optional VTOC
- ☐ Extended outline

PAGE FORMAT
- ☐ Sample pages and supporting descriptive notes

SCHEDULE AND RESOURCES
- ☐ Support services requirements
- ☐ Names of the reviewers
- ☐ Case study requirements
- ☐ Development schedule
- ☐ Production control forms
- ☐ Number of copies
- ☐ Distribution requirements

™ of Sandra Pakin & Associates, Inc.

 **Part 3**

Review

Review is a fundamental and necessary aspect of producing documentation that is properly targeted, easy-to-use, and easy-to-understand.

Reviewing at critical points during development enables you to make additions, corrections, and deletions before incurring the additional costs of the next development tasks. To plan and conduct reviews, you need review management skills.

Every document development project, regardless of size or complexity, requires the three DDM review tasks. These review tasks are:
- Task 4 - Review Document Plan and Commit to Writing
- Task 7 - Review Technical Detail
- Task 9 - Review Final Draft and Commit to Publication

The needs of the project may dictate additional reviews.

Chapters 6 and 7 discuss the review activities needed to manage reviews.

Chapter 6 - Managing the Review Process

Reviews are beneficial only when reviewers are carefully selected and briefed on their review responsibilities, when reviewers have a reasonable version of the document to review, and when review comments are accepted and used to improve the document. This chapter discusses how to manage the review of your documentation.

Chapter 7 - Field Testing

A field test is a selective or preliminary release of a document to actual users before final publication. This chapter discusses how to structure a field test so the documentation can be tried under actual use conditions.

Chapter 6

Managing the Review Process

Chapter 6
Managing the Review Process

In a successful project, the document produced is a synthesis of the writer's skill in planning and developing the contents and of the directions and insights provided by various types of reviewers. To be effective, however, review must be managed. Multiple reviewers are necessary to ensure that the document is reviewed from all viewpoints. Having several types of reviews helps you produce a complete and accurate document.

If you limit review to a consideration of only the first draft, for example, you will have no check on the scope, direction, or accuracy of the material after the rewrite. If you postpone review until the document is ready for publication, you may have done extensive development of sections that are inherently defective. Parts of your final draft may be inaccurate, ineffective for the audience, or outside the planned scope of the document.

Management of the review process begins in project planning with the definition of review checkpoints in the development scenario. It also involves selecting reviewers and briefing them on review goals and ends with following through on review comments. This chapter discusses these review management responsibilities.

Identifying Reviewers

The selection of reviewers is critical to the success of review. First, reviewers must represent a range of viewpoints and second, all reviewers must be responsible and effective reviewers.

TYPES OF REVIEWERS   Although every type of reviewer does not participate in every review, the project should involve four types of reviewers:
- Technical reviewers
- User reviewers
- Management reviewers
- Editorial reviewers

Technical Reviewers   Most MIS material is technical in nature. A document intended for non-technical audiences should omit some of the technical detail and simplify technical explanation to suit the potential readers. It is essential that at least one reviewer have the technical background and expertise to ensure that all information is accurate and complete.

Technical reviewers can be members of the project team or others who understand the technical detail. They review at all development

℗ of Sandra Pakin & Associates, Inc.

stages and should check the accuracy of:

- Equipment and application explanations, overviews, and processing flows
- Figures and diagrams
- Explanations of forms, reports, and screens
- Procedures

User Reviewers

User reviewers represent the final audience. They should reflect the experience and training of that audience. Users review for the usefulness of the instructions in their business operations, the appropriateness of the language and examples, and the readability of the material.

Generally, users review the content planning and the text after the technical detail is confirmed. They should:

- Point out unexplained assumptions, incomplete explanations, and unsupported conclusions.
- Strengthen the organization to meet the information needs of the audience.
- Spot inconsistencies in the presentation.
- Identify terminology and explanations that are too technical.
- Identify glossary terms.
- Identify inaccuracies between the documentation and actual system use.

Management Reviewers

Management should approve the project plan for multi-document projects. Management approval is also necessary during two review tasks:

- Task 4 - Review Document Plan and Commit to Writing
- Task 9 - Review Final Draft and Commit to Publication

Management reviewers check for compatability with the strategic and long-range plans of the MIS department and company and approve additional resources for continued development.

Editorial Reviewers

Editors concern themselves with how the document looks and how it reads. Editors generally review only in the last stages of rewrite, when they edit the final text to ensure consistency, grammatical accuracy, and conformity to standards.

For materials where user reviewers are not readily available, such as materials prepared by vendors for customer audiences, editors can also review from a user perspective.

SELECTION CRITERIA

Since review plays such an important part in the development of a document, selection of informed, responsible reviewers is essential. The following guidelines should help you identify appropriate reviewers.

General Reviewer Selection

In addition to having the requisite knowledge, reviewers should represent a range of viewpoints. Also, your reviewers must:

- Respect deadlines. Particularly with a tight development schedule, reviewers should be people who organize their time well and are able to work against a deadline. Waiting for the return of reviewer comments can delay your entire development.
- Maintain focus. Various types of reviewers are necessary to review different aspects of the document. For example, users review for appropriate language and reasonable operating situations but do not specifically look for technical inaccuracies or errors in grammar and style. Those are the jobs of

the technical and editorial reviewers. Select reviewers who can stick to their review assignments.

- Cooperate with other reviewers. Not every review comment is applicable or appropriate. Reviewers should understand that you may have to compromise between their comments and those of other reviewers. You may not be able to use every one of their review comments.

Editor Selection   MIS documents, like all documents, have specialized editorial requirements. When seeking editing support, look for:

- Technical understanding.
- Experience in similar types of documentation. Editing newsletter articles, for example, is not a good background for editing a 100-page user's guide. The techniques for editing sustained and lengthy technical materials are different from editing short, less technical materials.
- Adequate time availability. To perform a good edit on a technical document, the editor must have sufficient sustained time to work on the project. A few hours free time here and there can only result in choppy, unprofessional editing.

If your department or company does not have editors available, consider asking a colleague with a penchant for detail, grammar, and spelling to edit your material. If the material is going to have a wide distribution or is directed to a critical audience, consider contracting with an editorial service to perform a professional edit.

Conducting Reviews

Once you have selected reviewers, it is your responsibility to make the most of each review. You can do this by:

- Preparing the review document properly.
- Briefing the reviewers on their review tasks.
- Making effective use of the review comments.

DOCUMENT PREPARATION   Too often a writer sabotages a good review by providing reviewers with a poorly prepared document to review. Do not submit anything less than your best effort at the current stage of development. Do not submit a document for review if you know what errors, misconceptions, and omissions it contains. Do not ask for review of a document that you as the writer can improve *without* reviewer input.

This does not mean reviewers need a publication-ready document for first draft review. It does mean the review copy must be complete, with all introductions and figures in place. Although the first draft does not need finished art for the figures, it should include sketches so reviewers can review text and figures together.

In addition to providing a complete version of the text and figures, the review copy must also be:

- Legible. Your reviewers deserve a freshly typed document or an unmarked printout.
- Referenceable. Reviewers should not have to guess at the contents or order of the document. The review copy should be complete with a table of contents, section tabs, and as much of the glossary as you have completed. If you are reviewing a section at a time, the review package should include the outline of other sections so reviewers can tell where missing in-

formation is going to be.

- Formatted like the final document. If the final draft will be typed, the review draft should be prepared in the same format. In this way, the final document is not a surprise to reviewers.

  For a typeset final draft, prepare at least two pages in the final format so reviewers can see what the final document will look like. If you are providing a draft of a brochure for review, include a copy of the layout so reviewers get an idea of the final presentation.

REVIEWER BRIEFINGS

In reviewer briefings, you explain the review goals for the type of review being conducted and provide general and specific review instructions.

Review Goals

As material moves through development, the focus of review of the material changes. To manage reviewers and the review process, you must brief your reviewers on the review goals for each kind of review. The following paragraphs summarize these goals. The checklist at the end of the chapter provides specific questions reviewers should answer as they review the material.

Project Plan Review. Management and technical reviewers usually review the project plan. They concentrate on whether the plan lists all documents and has designated the correct audiences and media. They also check the development requirements to confirm that needed resources can be provided.

Document Plan Review. The document plan review usually involves user, management, and technical reviewers.

- Users and management concentrate on the document's requirements statement to ensure that it states scope and direction of the document accurately and correctly identifies the audience. They review sample page formats for suitability.
- Technical reviewers concentrate on the text outlines to ensure that the organization allows for discussion of all topics at their proper place and in appropriate detail.

All reviewers should evaluate the schedule and resources to ensure that they can commit to these development requirements.

Plans are internal working documents and reviewers should not comment on the writing style.

First Draft Review. Review of the first draft calls for technical reviewers. It is basically a review for technical accuracy and completeness. The wording of individual sentences is *not* an issue. But reviewers should identify unclear sentences and paragraphs.

Management and users generally do not review the first draft. You may want management or user reviewers if the material is particularly sensitive, if you are concerned about the appropriateness of the level of detail being presented, or if the material covers user procedures.

Ensuring that the material is accurate is the key goal of first draft review. Direct your reviewers to review the text to ensure that the discussion fulfills your scope and purpose. Reviewers should also verify that the emphasis of the discussion sections is appropriate and that procedural instructions are properly ordered and complete.

During first draft review, technical reviewers should also review all

™ of Sandra Pakin & Associates, Inc.

forms, screens, reports, and other graphics to be sure that:

- All field headings are accurate.
- The most current version is used.
- All explanations are complete.

Rewrite Review. By the time you reach rewrite review, you should have corrected gross technical errors and added all necessary detail. The writing style should be clear and uniform. If you had a lot of corrections to make or if you intend to field test, you may need more than one rewrite review. Also, if you plan to have the final version typeset, you may want a second review of your rewrite.

Technical reviewers reread everything and particularly review:

- All material that changed from the previous version.
- All graphics and figures for accuracy, placement, and pertinence.

User reviewers should read the text for appropriate language, level of detail, and effectiveness of user procedures. User reviewers should note any figures or graphics that are too technical, not appropriate, or confusing.

For typeset material, all reviewers should ensure that the typeset version is an accurate translation of the typed version.

Editorial Review. Editing takes place after the text has incorporated rewrite comments, but before it goes for field testing or final production. The editor ensures that the text, headings, and graphics are consistent and adhere to established standards.

The editor should always discuss with you any change that might affect the meaning of a sentence. Never let an editor submit work directly to production.

Final Draft Review. This review ensures that you made all changes, placed all figures properly, and numbered and assembled all pages properly to ensure the flow of the text. Either the writer or the editor can perform the final draft review.

For highly sensitive or technical documents, additional reviewers should review the document as a final check on content and accuracy. In this case, stress that the final review is *technical only.* Once the pages are formatted and the illustrations are in place, it is too late for style changes or unnecessary text additions. Only errors in technical information should be corrected. If the document requires extensive changes, return to the rewrite task.

Review Instructions Reviewer briefings are done in two stages: General instructions when you select the reviewers and specific instructions when you distribute the document for review.

General Instructions. A review meeting is a good way to discuss the review objectives if all your reviewers are at a single site. In the meeting, you can discuss:

- Scope and purpose of the document or documents.
- Review criteria for each document.
- Specific responsibilities, particularly where they are unique. User reviewers, for example, should be alerted to their responsibility for identifying all language that would be new or difficult for the user audience and all examples and procedures that the reader might not understand.
- Timing and procedures for review.
- All reviewer questions.

If you cannot meet with reviewers, circulate a memo that provides reviewers with general review guidelines, as shown in Figure 6.1.

MEMORANDUM   X-CO, Inc.

TO   Jack LaMotte, Janice Townsend, Chuck Mantrus,
          Howard Marcus, Shirley Ueber

FROM Sharon Goodfellow

DATE June 1, 1982

SUBJECT General Instructions for Reviewing Order Entry
             Documentation

Thank you for agreeing to review the Order Entry documentation.
As I complete drafts, I will forward them to you.

The following general guidelines provide suggestions for
reviewing the documentation. In addition to these guidelines,
the material to be reviewed is accompanied by a cover memo,
alerting you to some specific items to consider in your review.
Please mark your comments directly on the draft. You can also
use the back side of the pages to add additional comments.

Please consider:

o   <u>Technical Accuracy</u>. Does the information presented
     accurately reflect the current status of the system?

o   <u>Completeness</u>.   Is all technical information, known at this
     time, accounted for?

o   <u>Reasonableness of Organization</u>. Does the material follow a
     clear, easy-to-understand logical pattern?

o   <u>Appropriateness of Approach to Audience</u>. Does the material
     use vocabulary understandable to the specified audience
     without condescending? Are the graphics appropriate to the
     audience?

Although the editor will do a thorough language and grammar
review, it would help my rewriting efforts if you also flagged
language and presentation problems, such as unclear statements,
confusing explanation, and awkward language.

Figure 6.1 General review guidelines

Specific Instructions. Accompany every review document by a memo of specific review instructions on the purpose and goals of the review at this stage. This memo should also note specific changes from a previous draft if they are pertinent to the review. In addition, whenever appropriate, you should write special instructions for each type of reviewer. For example, during final review before publication, it is assumed that style problems have been solved. You should instruct reviewers to concentrate on eliminating errors and assuring that the text has the correct format.

The sample memos of Figure 6.2 are for two different types of reviewers for the same document, an in-house marketing brochure describing an order entry application.

MEMORANDUM   X−CO, Inc.

TO   Chuck Mantrus, Branch Relations Director

FROM   Sharon Goodfellow *S.G*

DATE   June 21, 1982

SUBJECT   Product Description Brochure − Order Entry Application

Enclosed is a draft of the four-page brochure describing our
order entry application. Jack LaMotta and Janice Townsend
reviewed an earlier draft and I have incorporated their
corrections.

Also enclosed is a copy of the requirements statement from the
document plan to remind you of the projected audience and scope
of the brochure.

Please review the brochure for the following:

o   Appropriateness to projected audience

o   Clarity of the description from the prospect´s viewpoint

o   Reasonableness of organization

o   Completeness of the description in anticipating possible
     questions

We want this brochure to fulfill our marketing needs. As our
chief liaison with current users, you should be able to provide
us with good feedback on this draft before we commit to
publication.

I´ve scheduled a review meeting to collect final changes and
approve the final draft for production for June 30 at 3:00 in
the MIS conference room. Jack, Janice, Howard Marcus, and
Shirley Uebner will also join us.

MEMORANDUM   X−CO, Inc.

TO   Jack LaMotta, Janice Townsend

FROM   Sharon Goodfellow *S.G*

DATE   June 13, 1982

SUBJECT   Product Description Brochure − Order Entry Application

Enclosed is the first draft of the four-page brochure describing
the order entry application.

Please review it for:

o   Technical Accuracy
o   Completeness
o   Reasonableness of organization
o   Appropriateness to audience

And pay special attention to the following:

o   Is the product use summary accurate?
o   Are the features accurately described?
o   Is the environment section clear?
o   Are the source and extent of our support accurately stated?

I´ve reserved conference room A on June 20 at 3:00 for us to
meet and go over your comments.

Figure 6.2 Memos of specific review instructions

Using Review Comments

Probably the most important factor in achieving *continued* success in review is the way you use the review comments. You must be an egoless writer to benefit from reviews.

It is easy for a writer to become defensive and sensitive about review comments. To approach the review with the right attitude, consider all development drafts as temporary. Be prepared to make changes to the document. Save your pride for the final product.

Read and listen to all review comments objectively. Later, reflect on the comments and decide whether they are valid. If they are not valid or not appropriate for your document, do not use them, but note the reasons why on the review copy.

INCORPORATING
REVIEW COMMENTS

After each review, prepare a correction copy from the individual review copies. Including all corrections in one correction copy avoids:
- Having conflicting corrections.
- Overlooking important changes.
- Dealing with the same corrections more than once.

When review comments indicate that the material is too difficult, too technical, not complete enough, or superfluous, do not be afraid to rewrite, change the writing plan, or restructure as needed. Development should change and improve the document.

OTHER USES FOR
REVIEW COMMENTS

When review begins on the first draft, start a word list of glossary terms. During early reviews you have the best opportunity to identify those words and terms that are difficult for reviewers. So be particularly aware of words that reviewers question or do not use properly in review discussions.

Be open to suggestions. A peripheral function of reviewing a user's guide, for example, is that it gives users another opportunity besides the business system design to see the proposed screens, reports, and procedures. You make documentation review do double work by profiting from valid review criticism of screens, reports, and procedures.

Following Up with Reviewers

After the review is over and you have prepared a correction copy, meet with reviewers to discuss their comments and recommendations. At such a meeting, you can work out conflicts on the spot and eliminate the need to check back with reviewers on contested points. The meeting also gives you an opportunity to explain to reviewers how their review is changing the document.

As a follow-up to the meeting or if a meeting is not feasible, it is a good idea to send a post-review memo to all reviewers, detailing:
- Nature of changes being made to the document.
- Length of time for corrections.
- Role of reviewers in the next review activity.

Questions for Reviewers

Producing an effective reader-directed document requires various levels of planning, development, *and* review. Effective review begins with the selection of good reviewers and is reinforced by good

® of Sandra Pakin & Associates, Inc.

management of the review process, including review follow-up.

The following checklist suggests questions that reviewers should answer during the various reviews.

PROJECT PLAN REVIEW
For the project design section:
- ☐ What documents are missing from the document list?
- ☐ Is the document list well structured?
- ☐ Are audience descriptions for each document correct and complete?
- ☐ Is medium for each document appropriate?
- ☐ Will the basic format be applicable to all the documents in the list? If not, what variations are required?
- ☐ Do the style guidelines make sense for this project?
- ☐ Do you agree with the graphic approach?

For the development requirements section:
- ☐ Are the document priorities accurate?
- ☐ Have all needed reviews and reviewers been accounted for?
- ☐ Is the review structure suitable?
- ☐ Can all production requirements be satisfied?
- ☐ Does the development scenario list all necessary checkpoints?

DOCUMENT PLAN REVIEW
For the requirements statement:
- ☐ Does the subject overview adequately summarize the subject of the document?
- ☐ Are the document scope and purpose reasonable and what you expected?
- ☐ Is the description of the audiences of the document complete and accurate?
- ☐ Will the audiences use the material in the ways described?

For the outline:
- ☐ Does the document organization make sense? Are sections properly subordinated?
- ☐ What topics are missing from the outline?
- ☐ Is the content of the extended outline accurate and complete?
- ☐ Is the level of detail indicated by the extended outline appropriate? Is more needed? Less?

For the page format:
- ☐ Is all the needed control information present, such as manual name, page number, issue date, section and subject designations?
- ☐ Is the type readable and not all capital letters, italics, or OCR type?
- ☐ Is line length less than six inches?
- ☐ Are the margins wide enough?
- ☐ Do you like the overall appearance?

For the schedule and resources:
- ☐ Is the development schedule reasonable? Are you assured that the target dates can be met?
- ☐ Can the support services requirements be satisfied?

℗ of Sandra Pakin & Associates, Inc.

☐ Will the selected reviewers be responsible and effective reviewers?

☐ Have all necessary reviewers been included?

FIRST DRAFT REVIEW

☐ What are the strengths of the document? Its weaknesses?

☐ Does the organization make sense?

☐ Have the purpose and usefulness of the subject been conveyed?

☐ What information is missing?

☐ Are procedural instructions properly ordered and complete?

☐ Are descriptions complete and accurate?

☐ Do the introductions properly introduce the subject matter or do they simply repeat the detail sections?

☐ What sentences or paragraphs are unclear and need rewriting?

For the forms, screens, reports, and other graphics:

☐ Are all field headings accurate?

☐ Is the most current version used?

☐ Are explanations complete?

REWRITE REVIEW

☐ Are the language and presentation right for the audience?

☐ Are graphics accurate, properly placed, and pertinent?

☐ Is the technical information complete and accurate?

☐ Is the writing clear, simple, and uniform?

EDITORIAL REVIEW

Have the following items been corrected:

☐ Grammar

☐ Spelling and capitalization

☐ Punctuation

☐ Poorly expressed sentences

Have the following items been checked:

☐ Compliance with standards

☐ Table of contents and text headings

☐ Page numbers in table of contents

☐ Page numbers of index items (spot-check)

FINAL REVIEW

☐ Were all changes made?

☐ Are all figures in the right places?

☐ Are all pages numbered and assembled in their right order?

☐ Are all pages included?

Chapter 7
Field Testing

Chapter 7
Field Testing

Having an accurate and attractively packaged user's guide is not enough to ensure its success. When documentation does not present conceptual, procedural, or operational information in ways readers can relate to, they ignore it. Including users on your review team is one way to improve the user orientation of your materials. Field testing is another way to ensure user acceptance and effectiveness of the document in the operating environment.

In field testing, you release a draft of the document for use by a typical user audience in an actual work situation. You then monitor the usability of the document by this audience. Particularly in extensive documentation projects, such as the development of user's and operator's guides, field testing has many advantages. In addition to testing the material under working conditions, field testing can:

- Expose any important omissions of definitions, descriptions, and procedures.
- Test the material for audience perspective — that it uses their terminology, reflects accurate and approved work practices, and distinguishes between important and secondary procedures.
- Generate user acceptance of the documentation because end users have helped to develop their own materials.
- Provide documentation for the user acceptance test of the system.

Field Test Timing

The system should be available for use during the field test, so computer procedures can be tested. Thus, a good time for the field test is during system test or pilot test. It can also take place during user acceptance test. For limited projects, plan on a minimum of three weeks for a field test. Longer, more complicated projects may require six to eight weeks.

In projects with limited development time, you can coordinate the field test with initial release of the document. The field test version serves as the documentation until the test is over and you have collected the comments, made the corrections, and released the final version.

Selecting Field Test Participants

Select as field testers people who will actually use the document in practice. If the document is for data entry clerks, data entry clerks should be the primary field testers. Secondary audiences can also participate in the field test.

In addition to performing the same job as the intended audience, field testers must have the experience assumed by the document. If the material is for trainees, some field testers must be trainees. If the material assumes prerequisites such as training or familiarity with other documents, testers must have the same prerequisites for a good test. In other words, field testers should represent a cross-section of the audience and should:

- Represent a broad enough sampling of the audience to make the test realistic.
- Use the document in an actual work situation.

SIMULATED FIELD TEST

If you have no access to users, you can simulate a field test. Simulating a field test means that reviewers outside the development team assume the role of typical users. For an operator's guide, for example, clerks or secretaries can act as beginning data entry operators reading the instructions and performing the procedures described in the guide.

Preparing the Field Test Copy

Within reason, the field test version should look like the final copy. The matrix of Figure 7.1 summarizes the differences between the field test version and the final version.

ELEMENT	FIELD TEST VERSION	FINAL VERSION
Graphics	Readable sketches	Finished drawings
Format	Typed	Typed or typeset
Section Tabs	Yes	Yes
Table of Contents	Detailed contents in front of manual	Detailed contents in front of manual, plus chapter contents after each section tab
Glossary	Yes	Yes
Index	No	Yes

Figure 7.1 Differences between field test and final versions

In preparing the field test version, be sure it has:
- Complete text. The most recent, updated version of the text should be neatly typed in the established page format.
- All graphics. All illustrations, charts, and graphics should be reduced and inserted in the proper text position. The artwork does not have to be in final form, but graphics and explanations should be together. It is not a true field test when figures are omitted, printed on separate pages, or grouped together at the back of the document.
- Proper packaging. All pages in the field test version should be numbered. It should be distributed in a binder with tabs between sections and should include all available reference aids — at a minimum, the table of contents with page numbers and the glossary.

On the title page, identify the document as field test material and add a statement, such as:

> *This Field Test Version is tentative and preliminary and is for discussion only. No copies of this material should be made or distributed. At the completion of the field test, this material must be returned to J. Smith, Field Test Coordinator (X9999).*

Briefing Participants on the Test

In the field test, as in every type of review, the reviewers must know their review responsibilities. Although the briefing guidelines presented in Chapter 6 apply, there are some specific briefing considerations for a field test.

With anything but a very limited internal field test, testers are probably scattered. This makes the use of a review meeting for introductory remarks difficult or impossible. As a result, written instructions for the field testers must be clear and specific. The memo shown in Figure 7.2 outlines the field testing procedure and provides the reviewers with some specific questions to answer.

Occasionally, areas in the documentation require specific review. Field test versions of the document should, then, call attention to the material so the reviewer does not forget to give it careful attention. You can insert special review notes to ask specific questions of the reviewer — for example, questioning whether a figure is too technical.

Providing Reviewer Feedback

Field test reviewers' efforts should always be acknowledged. A personal note or letter is generally most effective. You may also acknowledge field testers in an acknowledgment section of the document's preface. For example:

> *We appreciate the participation of the Chicago office in a field test of an earlier version of this user's guide.*

MEMORANDUM   BCA, Limited

TO   Distribution List

FROM   J. Smith, Field Test Coordinator (ext. 9999) J.S.

DATE   May 17, 1982

SUBJECT Super System User's Guide - Field Test Instructions

As a user of the SUPER System, you can provide valuable information on the effectiveness and usefulness of the user's guide.

The field test will last approximately four weeks and is made up of three parts:

1. Pre-test meeting on June 1, 1982 to discuss the materials.

2. Your review of the materials and try-out of the procedures and forms.

3. Debriefing meeting on June 29, 1982 to discuss your findings.

Please mark your copy of the material with any questions, comments, or corrections you may have. In addition, please answer the following questions on a separate page.

o   What sections were difficult to understand?

o   Was it easy to find information?

o   What terms need explaining?

o   What information was missing and needed?

o   How can we improve the troubleshooting section to help you resolve errors more easily?

o   What did you like best about the document? What least?

Please bring your marked up copy, the responses to the above questions, and any other documentation notes to the June 29 debriefing meeting.

Thank you.

Figure 7.2 Instruction memo to all field testers

Questions for Field Test Participants

To conduct the field test, circulate the document to a typical user audience. The important difference between the field test version and final version is the content change that results from the experience of actual users reviewing the material in real situations.

From the field test, you discover explanations to clarify, procedural steps to include or improve, troubleshooting techniques to cover, and sections needing graphics. You may even discover material that is too technical and information that can be deleted. Whatever your findings, the final document is more user-oriented as a result of a field test in the user environment.

Consider the following when you prepare questions to be answered by field test participants:

- ☐ What sections were difficult to understand?
- ☐ Was it easy to find information?
- ☐ What are the errors?
- ☐ What terms need explaining?
- ☐ What procedures were hard to follow?
- ☐ Was any information missing?
- ☐ What did you like best about the document? What least?

™ of Sandra Pakin & Associates, Inc.

 **Part 4**

Writing

Inexperienced writers make three mistakes. They begin writing before they have planned the document. They write the introductions before writing the detail sections. And they stop writing after the first draft.

With the DDM, planning and plan review are preparation for writing. When you sit down to write the first draft, it is structured, planned writing. You start writing the detail sections first and you always rewrite before publication. Writing skills are needed to perform the two writing tasks:

- Task 5 - Write First Draft
- Task 8 - Rewrite and Complete Graphics

Concurrently with the first draft writing, you develop illustrations and graphics. When you reach Task 8, you are ready to unify text and graphics into a cohesive, effective document.

Chapters 8, 9, and 10 discuss the writing activities needed to complete these tasks:

Chapter 8 - Preparing a First Draft

This chapter explains how to move from a document outline to a document draft. The discussion describes some basic writing principles and provides some tips to make the writing effort easier. It also provides specific ways to handle various types of writing, such as procedures and descriptions of forms, screens, and reports.

Chapter 9 - Rewriting

Rewriting is based on your personal review of your draft and on comments from your reviewers. This chapter discusses how to approach the rewrite of your first draft and how to fashion your final draft.

Chapter 10 - Preparing Reference Aids

Most MIS documents are used as references. They are seldom read straight through. You improve the effectiveness of your document by providing appropriate reference aids, including tables of contents, headings, glossary, and index. This chapter provides specific guidelines for preparing these reference aids.

Chapter 8

Preparing a First Draft

DDM™ **Chapter 8**
Preparing a First Draft

The hardest task in the entire documentation development process can be writing the first draft. One purpose of planning is to simplify this first writing task by gathering and structuring the information and establishing guidelines for the presentation of the material. After review and correction of the document plan, writing can begin.

You can ease the first draft writing process by following the order of development given in this chapter:
- Review the document plan and project writing guide.
- Apply the basic writing principles.
- Write the detail sections first and note the figures and illustrations needed.
- Write the general sections.
- Prepare a reader's comment form.

Review the Document Plan

The document plan is the specification for the document. It is your guide to the purpose, audience, content, and format of the document you are to write. The document plan helps you determine the level of detail needed and what topics to stress. For example, if you are writing a self-study guide for beginning operators, you may want to stress the day-to-day use of the system, since this is the information a beginner needs the most.

Read the audience definition. Be sure you can imagine a member of this audience. You may want to select a member of the audience whom you know and write the draft as though you were formally explaining the information to that one person. If you do not know anyone in the audience, you should interview some users and see where and how they work.

The project writing guide contains the text standards for developing the document. It will help the typist if you follow the text standards as you prepare your draft.

Apply Basic Writing Principles

Four writing principles simplify writing the first draft:
- Expand the extended outline.
- Write for the audience.
- Do not belabor individual sentences.
- Use a straightforward style.

EXPAND THE EXTENDED OUTLINE The extended outline specifies what a section should contain. Using this as a basis, create complete sentences that express the information. For each topic in the outline, ask yourself what more you need to say or explain. Write additional sentences (forming paragraphs) to meet these requirements.

For example, the extended outline below is for a section introducing the Financial System data base. Figure 8.1 shows the first draft from this outline, written for planners in the corporate financial office who will be using the system.

> 1. *The Financial System data base*
>   a. *Data base is organized to reflect the financial structure of the corporation and its reporting requirements. It includes:*
>   (1) *Corporate organization structure*
>   (2) *Account data*
>   (3) *Accounting structure*
>   b. *Data base includes actual operating data and budget data*
>   c. *Data base is used to consolidate operating data totals throughout the corporation and to prepare monthly and year-end schedules and statements.*
>   d. *Major benefits include:*
>   (1) *Serves as a foundation for continuity and provides timely information*
>   (2) *Serves as a collection point for historical data for analysis*

Figure 8.1 is the writer's first attempt to fill in the outline. It is a reasonable first draft, but it is *not* finished writing. When the first draft is complete, rewriting can begin. Figure 9.2 shows the writer's critical reading of the draft and Figure 9.3 shows how he rewrote the draft as a result.

Change the Outline If Necessary As you write, you may find that the outline needs changing. You may have designated more sections than you need to explain the material, or some sections may need re-ordering.

The document plan is a working document and changes are common. However, you should annotate a copy of the plan with your changes so these decisions are recorded. It is not necessary to submit the revised plan for review.

Follow the Page Format If you follow the text format, you get an impression of the final appearance of your material. The format may also need modifying as you apply text to it. You should annotate the page format with any changes so the decisions you make can be part of the history file for the document. If your document is part of a series, be sure that your changes to the format do not affect the continuity of the series. Compromises may be necessary.

WRITE FOR THE AUDIENCE Every audience — whether it is programmers, computer operators, end users, or executive management — has its own vocabulary, interests, and needs. Writing for the audience means writing in a style and vocabulary easily understood by the audience. It means including only information that the audience needs.

A data entry operator, for instance, is not interested in a design discussion of the reasons why screens were sequenced in a particular way. Rather, the operator needs to know how to get to a screen and the screens accessible from it. Similarly, the batch operator does not need to know how to use the various reports he prints and distributes.

```
                                        FINANCIAL SYSTEM OVERVIEW
                                        Financial System Data Base


    FINANCIAL SYSTEM DATA BASE

    The Financial System data base is the means of providing a
    single source for financial account information, which might be
    actual operating data or budget data. The actual operating data
    goes back to 1970 and the budget data is for the current budget
    year, although at a later time historical data for years prior
    to 1970 may be input if corporate makes a decision that this
    information would be of value to the corporation.

    DATA BASE ORGANIZATION

    The data base is organized to reflect the financial structure of
    the corporation and its requirements.  There are three kinds of
    information which are stored in the data base:

    o    Corporate organizational structure, which is the
         hierarchical arrangement of entities within the
         Corporation.

    o    Account data by entity.  This is the actual monthly
         operating data and budget data for each entity identified
         in the organization.

    o    Accounting structure includes the accounts for which data
         is collected and the form and order of reporting those
         accounts.

    USES OF THE DATA BASE

    All Financial System functions add to and/or use data in the
    data base.  Data input for reporting locations is consolidated
    automatically by the Financial System to form consolidated
    totals, initially up to the group level, then to the division
    level and finally (on approval of the division) to Corporate
    headquarters.

    The data base serves as the foundation for continuity and
    timeliness of financial information.  After budget data has been
    entered, it becomes available for comparing to actual operating
    data on monthly statements.  Reports prepared by the Financial
    System reflect the latest financial information and the ability
    to restate historical data to reflect current operations and
    organization makes it possible to produce reports that
    accurately compare periods.  In addition to supplying data for
    the preparation of budget schedules and actual operating
    statements, the data base will supply data for various
    statistical and financial analysis programs.




    draft (3/24/82)                                              1
```

Figure 8.1 *First draft of writing from the extended outline*

A technical audience charged with maintaining a system would be disappointed reading only a general description of the programs rather than seeing program flow diagrams also.

To reach the audience, you must use their vocabulary to provide information that relates to their needs and interests. For example, consider the following two paragraphs written for a company newsletter. Each introduces some aspect of the XYZ terminal, but the first is written from a management perspective, the second from an operator's point of view.

> *The first installation of the XYZ intelligent terminal resulted in a 68% timesharing cost savings for the Boston office. At this rate, Boston will recover its initial installation costs in 1.8 years. Considering the rising rate of timesharing charges and Boston's increased use of timesharing over the past year, however, Boston's manager Frederick H. Golf projects that, with the XYZ terminal, his office will achieve actual cost savings in the first year.*

Boston's operator Jan Brooks reports that data entry is much easier on the new XYZ intelligent terminal. Most of her data entry and validation can be done on the terminal without complicated timesharing dial-up or waiting for a timesharing connection. Jan reports that she particularly likes the terminal's display screen because "I can see what I'm doing."

Each of these paragraphs is directed to a specific but different audience. The problem with much writing is that it uses either a management or the writer's point of view for every audience. It is essential to translate the material into the audience's point of view.

DO NOT BELABOR INDIVIDUAL SENTENCES A first draft is just that. It is your first attempt to write the words around your outline. This is the first time you will see whether your structure works. If it does not, you will be reorganizing and rewriting and the sentences are going to change anyway. Rewriting, which is essential to producing materials worth reading, is the time to select the perfect word, polish sentences, and refine paragraphs.

If you have trouble expressing a point, substitute the outline or commentary about what you want to say and move on with your writing. Chances are that when you review your material, you will know what to say and can fill in the gaps. If you cannot, talk over your problems with a colleague or one of your reviewers.

USE A STRAIGHTFORWARD STYLE A logical, well-structured document organization is the beginning of a straightforward style. As you fill in your outline with words, observe these rules for simplifying your writing:
- Use action verbs.
- Get to the point.
- Stick to the point.

Use Action Verbs Action verbs show movement. They direct the reader to do something. Look at these pairs of sentences:

NOT: *The data entry clerk is responsible for entering the data.*
BUT: *The data entry clerk enters the data.*
NOT: *The terminal screen is the place where information is displayed.*
BUT: *The terminal screen displays information.*

Get to the Point Short sentences do not signify lack of substance. Better than eliminating unnecessary words during rewriting, learn to avoid writing them in the first place. Ask yourself what is the *minimum* number of words needed to make the reader understand. Compare these sentences:

NOT: *The purpose of this file is to provide the capability for storing passwords.*
BUT: *This file stores passwords.*
NOT: *This manual should be used as a reference to essential system information.*
BUT: *This is a reference manual.*

Stick to the Point When you know a subject well, it is difficult to limit your writing to the information the audience needs. It is a great temptation to provide tangential information. For example, the following explanation for turning on a terminal provides too much information for an operator's or user's guide. It is also unnecessarily technical and complicated.

NOT: *To power on the XYZ terminal, switch the POWER toggle to the ON position and press the RETURN key. When the switches make the ON connection, a message goes through the switching center, putting the terminal online. Pressing RETURN brings up the sign-on message panel on the CRT display.*

BUT: *To turn on the XYZ terminal:*
1. Push the POWER switch to ON.
2. Press the RETURN key.
The system responds with the following sign-on message:

Welcome to XYZ.

Enter your system ID and application code to begin processing.

Operators need to know what to do and what they will see. They do not need to know what happens in the equipment. Also, they do not need to deal with technical terms and unnecessary jargon, such as: *power on, toggle, panel.*

Write the Detail Sections

Start writing the detail sections first because these are the easiest to write. They are factual and straightforward and usually do not require summarizing and narrative techniques.

Of the detail sections, you should write the descriptive sections first, then the procedural sections. For example, if you are writing a user's guide for an online decision support system, you should write the input form, screen, and report descriptions first and then the procedural sections.

While you are writing, you should make notes or sketches of the illustrations you plan to use. Also, make notes about general points to go into an introductory section. And finally, compile a word list for the project writing guide which includes your spelling or use of technical terms — for example, how you spell *logon (logon, log on, or log-on).*

WRITING DESCRIPTIONS

Your outline specifies what to describe. You may describe every field or only unique fields. For example, you would probably not describe name and telephone extension fields on an input form unless there was something special or unique about how to fill in this information. Often, forms, screens, and reports have common fields, such as customer name and number for an order entry system. Your outline may indicate that these common fields should be explained once in an introductory section.

Form, Screen, and Report Descriptions

Your format plan specifies the format for form, screen, and report descriptions. Figure 8.2 shows a good format for descriptions. Your writing task is to fill in the format with words.

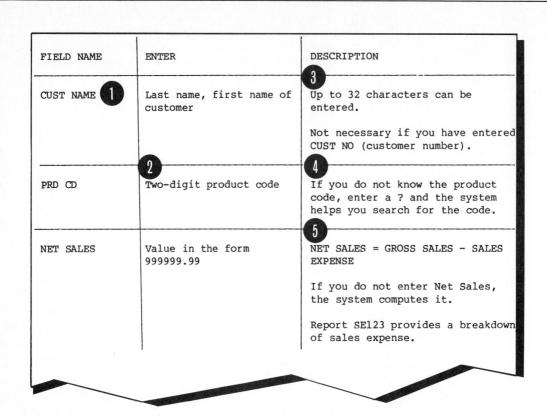

Figure 8.2 *Format for form, screen, or report descriptions*

❶ Write the name exactly the way it appears on the form, screen, or report.

❷ If the field name is an abbreviation, include a spelled-out version of the abbreviation in the description.

❸ Give the size constraints or special characteristics of the field.

❹ Provide useful information. Do not start the description with the words "This field (or this column)." Tell what data the field or column contains. If the description is self-evident, say nothing but show an example.

❺ If a field is the result of a calculation, give the formula.

Equipment Descriptions
Describe equipment on a need-to-know basis and use illustrations to show features and controls. Figure 8.3 shows an equipment illustration and its relationship to the text.

WRITING PROCEDURES
Procedures are directions for performing some task — for example, correcting errors, logging on to a system, placing an order. Procedures may involve one person or several. All steps may be performed in order, or steps may be performed only when certain conditions exist.

What procedures have in common is action. They tell people how to do things. And so they must be written in a directive, easy-to-follow style. This means action verbs and short sentences. All information needed to perform the task correctly must be provided. For example, in a procedure to ready the disk drive for operation, the following is inadequate:

INADEQUATE: *Place the disk on the drive and turn the drive on.*

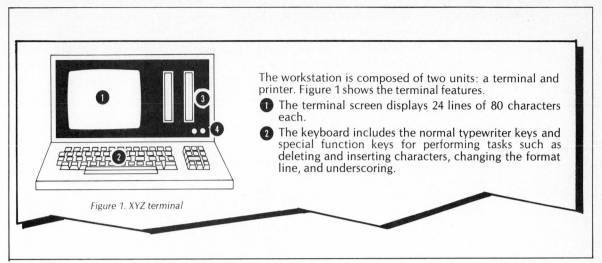

The workstation is composed of two units: a terminal and printer. Figure 1 shows the terminal features.

1 The terminal screen displays 24 lines of 80 characters each.

2 The keyboard includes the normal typewriter keys and special function keys for performing tasks such as deleting and inserting characters, changing the format line, and underscoring.

Figure 1. XYZ terminal

Figure 8.3 *Using illustrations for equipment descriptions*

This direction assumes that the reader knows how to place the disk on the disk drive and how to turn the drive on. But since this is the subject of the procedure, the following would be more appropriate:

IMPROVED: *1. Open the disk cabinet drawer.*
2. Slide the disk cartridge into the slot, with the arrow on the cartridge pointing in.
3. Close the disk cabinet drawer.
4. Press the POWER button to turn on the disk drive.

The direction "Place the disk on the drive and turn the drive on" would work as part of a summary procedure for system start up.

Procedure Based on Existing Conditions

Often procedural steps require that some condition exist before a step is performed, and performing that step has a definite result. In the example of readying the disk drive, assume the cabinet drawer will not open if the drive is already on. At the end, the drive is not ready until the green ready indicator lights up. A three-column format, as shown in Figure 8.4, helps clarify the procedure and explains this additional information.

CONDITION	STEP	RESULT
Power is on. Power is off.	1. Press the POWER button to turn the power off. 2. Open the disk cabinet drawer. 3. Slide the disk cartridge into the slot, with the arrow on the cartridge pointing in. 4. Close the disk cabinet drawer. 5. Press the POWER button to turn the power on.	Green READY indicator lights up within 30 seconds.

Figure 8.4 *Three-column format for procedures*

Procedures in Playscript

Some procedures involve interactions among several people or departments. The playscript format is ideal for that. Created by Leslie H. Matthies, the playscript procedure stresses the importance of teamwork by assigning specific roles and a sequence for execution of work. Figure 8.5 shows how the procedure for conducting a structured walk-through is described using playscript.

PROCEDURES FOR CONDUCTING A STRUCTURED WALK-THROUGH

Responsibility	*Action*
Programmer/analyst	1. Arranges and schedules a time within the next two weeks for a structured walk-through.
	2. Collects, reproduces, and distributes his design or code to selected reviewers. (Management is excluded from the review team, to encourage openness and frankness.)
Reviewers	3. At the meeting, appoint one member recording secretary.
	4. Comment on the completeness, accuracy, and general quality of the programmer/analyst's work.
	5. Express major concerns, if any, about the work product, and identify areas for potential follow-up.
Programmer/analyst	6. Walks the reviewers through the work product in enough detail that the major concerns expressed earlier are either cleared up or retained for follow-up.
Recording secretary	7. Records for an action list all errors, discrepancies, exposures, and inconsistencies uncovered during the walk-through.
	8. Distributes copies of the handwritten action list to all reviewers immediately after the meeting.
Programmer/analyst	9. Resolves the points of concern on the action list.
	10. Notifies the reviewers of the actions taken.

Figure 8.5 Playscript procedure

As you can see from the figure, the two main features of playscript are:

• Clear delineation of who does what and when
• Action statements

The playscript procedure for a structured walk-through shows the flow of work. It tells the review team what must occur during a structured walk-through. But it does not tell how to select reviewers, how reviewers analyze the design or code, or how to uncover and resolve errors, discrepancies, and inconsistencies. A playscript procedure assumes the participants know their profession. It is not a substitute for a job description, a training program, or detailed instructions.

Playscript is best when the action is straightforward. If a number of conditions determine the next action, a procedure written in playscript becomes difficult to follow. However, if there are only a few conditions, they can be handled in playscript by using sub-steps. For example, in a check-cashing procedure:

> 4. a. *If the amount exceeds $100, call xxx for verbal authorization.*
>   b. *If the amount exceeds $1000, see xxx for signed authorization.*

Procedure for Using an Online Application

You can use a variation on the playscript procedure for procedures that involve interacting with a computer system. This is shown in Figure 8.6.

PROMPT OR DISPLAY	YOUR ACTION
USER ID PASSWORD NO SUCH USER Main Menu	1. Enter your user ID. 2. Enter your password. 3. Re-enter your password. You are locked out of the system if you enter the wrong password a second time. 4. Press the PF key corresponding to your selection. Follow the procedure for that activity.

Figure 8.6 Two-column format for online application procedures

If necessary, you can add a third column to the online procedure:
- Results, where you describe the result of the action.
- Notes, where you further explain or clarify the action.
- Error correction, where you discuss how to correct errors that might occur.

Screens depicting the entry sequence can be shown as illustrations.

Procedure Based on Several Decisions

Some procedures are followed only when certain conditions exist — troubleshooting, for example. You can write these up in an "If..., And If..., Then..." format, as shown in Figure 8.7.

IF...	AND IF...	THEN...
Paper light is on	There is still paper in the feeder	Be sure the paper is straight. Press the Reset key. Check the feed track for a jam or obstruction. Press the Reset key.
	The feed track is clear	Check that the pressure plate lever is forward. Press the Reset key.

Figure 8.7 Format for procedures based on several decisions

The order in which you present the problems in a troubleshooting section is not important. However, arrange the problems topically for easy reference.

Write the General Sections

Each detail section needs introductory material, chapters may need summaries, and the entire document needs a preface and an overview. For a report, the overview is the management summary. Again, when writing the general sections, work from least difficult to most difficult: from introductions for the detail sections to chapter summaries and then to the chapter and manual overviews.

INTRODUCTIONS TO DETAIL SECTIONS

Summary information should introduce each form, screen, report, and procedure. It is often helpful to use fixed headings to orient the reader.

Introducing Forms

Consider the following information for your form introductions.

USE: State the use of the form. What activity does it document? Why is it needed?

You can keep yourself focused on use if for your first draft you start this explanation with "Use this form to...." For example:

Use the project reporting form to record all billable work you perform for a project.

CONTENT: Summarize the content of the form. Say what general sections it has. For example:

The form has three parts: project identifying information, daily detail, usage codes.

PREPARED BY: State who prepares the form.

APPROVAL: State who approves the form.

DISPOSITION: List who gets the form or what is done with it.

WHEN TO SUBMIT: Provide the schedule for delivery of the form.

OTHER FORMS: List all forms (screens or reports) related to this one.

Introducing Screens

Consider the following information when introducing screens.

USE: State the use of the screen. What data entry, processing, or inquiry does it allow?

CONTENT: Summarize what the screen contains.

HOW ACCESSED: Explain what menu selection, PF key, or action causes this screen to appear.

NEXT SCREEN: Explain what you do when you have completed this screen. What screen is displayed?

RELATED DOCUMENTS: List all documents related to this screen. Is an input form used with the screen? Does the information displayed correspond to a printed report?

Introducing Reports   Consider the following information for your report introductions.

PURPOSE:	State why the report exists. What information needs does it satisfy?
DISTRIBUTION:	State who receives the report.
FREQUENCY:	Tell how often the report is distributed. How is it requested?
FEATURES:	Highlight some of the important contents of the report.
SORT ORDER:	Tell how the report is arranged or sorted.
RELATED REPORTS:	List all related reports. What reports, printed and online, are related to this one? For example, this may be a summary report with additional detail reports available.

Introducing Procedures   Consider the following information for your procedure introductions.

PURPOSE:	Explain what the procedure is designed to accomplish.
RESPONSIBILITY:	State who is responsible for carrying out the procedure.
TIMING:	State when this procedure should be done. How long does it take?
WHAT YOU NEED:	List the materials needed to complete the procedure.
WHEN YOU ARE DONE:	Explain what happens as a result of performing this procedure. Something may be up and running or a new procedure is ready to be performed.

CHAPTER SUMMARIES   Chapter summaries may take one of the following forms:
- Narrative paragraph or two restating the important information conveyed in the chapter.
- Checklist consolidating detail information covered in the chapter. For example, summarize a detailed procedure by presenting the key steps for those readers who know the detail but just need a reminder of the order of steps. This checklist information is also often good subject matter for a reference summary card.

CHAPTER OVERVIEWS   A chapter overview presents a preview of the content of the chapter to help orient the reader to its subject matter. Additionally, it may contain some general or overall information needed to understand the chapter organization. For example, the introduction to a chapter on screen descriptions could logically group the screens by type or function to give the reader a perspective as he reads the screen detail. It might provide some suggestions for more easily using the screens. The introduction would also include a description of how the chapter presents information on each screen, as shown in Figure 8.8.

Chapter overviews do not have to be long and they do not have to be labeled "Overview" or "Introduction." The fact that the information is first in the chapter is enough.

PREFACE   The preface gives the reader enough information to determine whether he should continue to read the book. The preface, which is

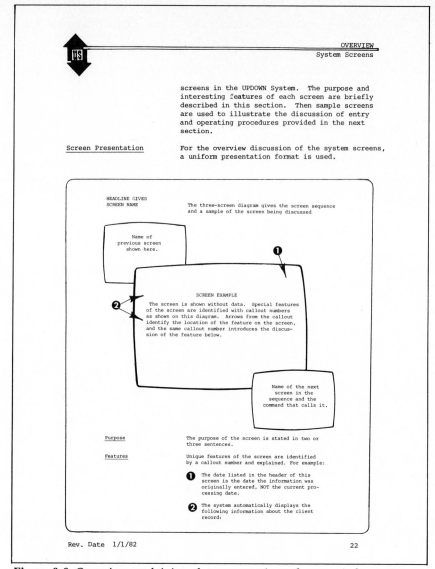

Figure 8.8 Overview explaining the presentation of screen information

usually one or two pages long, provides the following information:
- Purpose of the document
- Audience of the document
- Name and content of each chapter
- Available reference aids
- Prerequisite or corequisite material

Often the information in the preface is a rephrasing of the requirements statement of the document plan.

INTRODUCTION TO THE DOCUMENT

The introduction to the document sets the tone. It presents the direction of the material and provides the basic information the reader needs to understand the rest of the document. For example, the introduction to an application user's guide would include a description of the application processing flow. The introduction to a management report would be an executive summary highlighting the important information in the report.

Your outline should include the points you want to make in the introduction. Expand each\ of those points with a sentence or a paragraph. As you write, ask yourself what the reader needs to know about that point in order to understand the rest of the document. Then write only that. Remember, you have already written the details in the other sections.

Prepare the Reader's Comment Form

Including a reader's comment form is an easy way to solicit comments and corrections on a document after its distribution. A reader's comment form is provided at the end of this book.

Components of a First Draft

A first draft consists of the following written components:
- Preface
- Introduction to the document
- Chapters which contain:
  - Overview
  - Detailed information
  - Summary
- Reader's comment form

Write the chapter detail first, followed by the chapter overview and summary and finally the preface and introduction.

To prepare the first draft for technical review, add graphics (see Chapter 13, "Graphic Development") and a table of contents (see Chapter 10, "Preparing Reference Aids").

 **Chapter 9**
Rewriting

 **Chapter 9**
Rewriting

Writing a first draft takes a great deal of creative effort, but it is the beginning, not the end, of writing. You must rewrite your first draft to improve the writing style and to incorporate review comments and factual changes.

The document may go through several revision and review passes before approval for publication, but you follow the same basic procedure each time you rewrite. You:
- Identify what to rewrite.
- Fix writing problems.

Identifying What to Rewrite

You learn what rewriting is necessary from three sources:
- Your personal review
- Review comments
- Reports of factual changes

This section discusses what to expect from each of these sources.

YOUR PERSONAL REVIEW

Reread your draft to spot and correct problems before you distribute the draft for review. The checklist below can help you look at your writing critically and identify problems.

☐ Make notes to yourself on improvements you can make, such as "clarify," "needs an example," "needs an illustration," "order of steps."

☐ Mark any paragraph that extends more than a quarter of a page.

☐ Circle every semicolon.

☐ Mark any sentence longer than two lines.

☐ Circle or underscore with a wavy line long uncommon words, parenthetical expressions, every computer term for which you can substitute an everyday word, and the following:

    There is or There are

    In order to

    ....is to (such as "purpose is to")

    ....tion of the (such as "explanation of the")

    Herein, therein, or whereas

    Will

    That is or that are

    Which is or which are

☐ Check that every new term is explained.

☐ Check that the text refers to every figure.

☐ Check that each item in a list begins with the same type of word or phrase.

Figure 9.1 shows how the checklist was applied to the first draft shown in Figure 8.1, and Figure 9.2 shows the resulting rewrite. An explanation of the rewrite follows the figures.

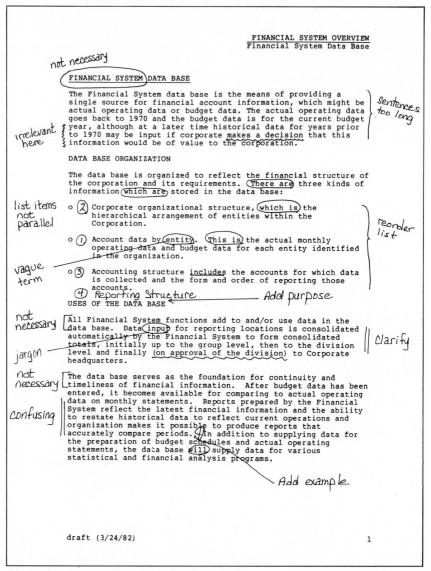

Figure 9.1 *Personal review of a first draft*

The rewrite of "Financial System Data Base" has defined and described the system in terms of kinds and uses of information. In its introduction, the first draft had two long sentences. They not only announced the topic, but also inserted supporting material properly belonging to the discussion that follows. The rewrite reduces the introduction to two short sentences.

The rewrite makes clear that the topic has two subtopics — "Information on the Data Base" and "Uses of the Data Base." For the first subtopic, the rewrite provides a parallel list of four items, going from operations data to the three kinds of information about structure. In the first draft, the list was neither parallel nor ordered. After the list,

```
                                          FINANCIAL SYSTEM OVERVIEW
                                                        Data Base



        structure.  This makes it possible to produce reports that
        accurately compare periods, despite any corporate
        reorganizations or account restructuring that might have
        occurred.

        For example, suppose a product line moves from one profit center
        to another.  The Financial System can restate last year's
        account data for these profit centers, as though the product
        line had moved last year.  In this way, yearly schedule
        comparisons have the same basis.
```

```
                                        FINANCIAL SYSTEM OVERVIEW
                                                      Data Base


     DATA BASE

     The Financial System data base provides a single source for
     financial account information.  It contains actual operating
     data since 1970 and the current year of budget data.

     INFORMATION ON THE DATA BASE

     The information on the data base supports the financial
     structure of the corporation and its reporting requirements.
     The data base contains:

     o    Account data -- the actual monthly operating and budget data
          for each profit center.

     o    Corporate organizational structure -- the hierarchical
          arrangement of profit centers, groups, and divisions.

     o    Accounting structure -- the accounts for which data is
          collected.

     o    Reporting structure -- the form and order of account
          reporting.

     Account data is used to prepare monthly and year-end budget
     schedules and actual operating statements.  The three types of
     structure information determine how account data is reported.
     Whenever the corporate financial structure changes, these data
     base structures can also be easily changed.

     USES OF THE DATA BASE

     The primary use of the data base is to provide up-to-date
     information for financial reports at all reporting levels --
     profit centers, groups, divisions, and the corporation as a
     whole.  Data is entered at each profit center.  Then following
     the organizational structure, the Financial System automatically
     combines data from all profit centers within a group to form
     consolidated group totals.

     Next, the Financial System consolidates group totals to form
     division totals, and finally combines division totals to form a
     corporate total.  Each month's statements show a comparison
     between budgeted and actual operating data at all reporting
     levels.  Besides supplying data for the preparation of budget
     schedules and actual operating statements, the data base
     supplies data for various statistical and financial analysis
     programs.

     Also, the Financial System can restate historical data from the
     data base in terms of the current organization and accounting


     FS User's Guide (5/1/82)                                     1
```

Figure 9.2 Rewrite following the comments in Figure 9.1

the rewrite briefly summarizes each type of information that the system stores.

The first draft had the same subtopic heading — "Uses of the Data Base" — as the rewrite. However, it used long, complicated sentences and had no obvious flow of thought. The rewrite has imposed a stronger organization on the information given in the first draft. *Primary, then, next, besides,* and *also* signal the pattern. The last paragraph supplies an example to clarify how the system uses its data.

The rewrite has sharpened the focus of the material. It has also eliminated the long, complicated, and sometimes unclear sentences of the first draft.

REVIEW COMMENTS Outside review is essential to help you rewrite. It is impossible to be totally objective about something you have written. Review comments cover accuracy, completeness, and user orientation as well as presentation. The checklist at the end of Chapter 6, "Reviewing Your Documentation," lists some of the questions reviewers answer during their review of the first draft.

Even though some reviewers rewrite sentences or write out the corrections or changes they think should be made, you must fit the corrections into the tone, style, and organizational structure of the piece you are writing. If necessary, discuss with the reviewer how you want to make the change or have him check the rewritten piece.

FACTUAL CHANGES Factual changes come from other sources besides major reviewers. For example, you may receive notices of system changes or may do additional information gathering because of gaps in the document. Review the writing plan or the text to determine where to incorporate these changes.

Consider what other changes are necessary because of the information you are adding. Do any tables or checklists change? Do benefits or introductory materials change? Must you revise summaries?

After making the changes, give them the same detailed review as the original writing.

Fixing Writing Problems

Most writing problems fall into one of these three categories:
- Long or complicated paragraphs
- Complicated sentences
- Difficult language

This section suggests ways to remedy problems in these categories.

PARAGRAPHS If paragraphs are too long, they appear difficult. If they are complicated, they provide too much information for easy understanding. To rewrite long paragraphs, look for a place to break the paragraph. This may be where you begin:
- A new thought
- Amplification of the thought
- Extended examples

Also, you can shorten your paragraphs by shortening the sentences that make up the paragraphs. For example:

NOT: *Time spent providing emergency maintenance, or service, be it by human and/or machine resources, cannot be planned as to the day or the length of time.*

BUT: *You cannot schedule emergency maintenance time.*

You can make complicated paragraphs more readable by turning them into tables. For example:

NOT: *The design of the package is reviewed by Quality Assurance to determine compliance with standards. The contract(s) will be reviewed (normally within three weeks) by the Law Department and reviewed (normally within four weeks) and endorsed by the Data Processing Steering Committee. Signed approval of the acquisition and contract will be by the department head for items under $100,000 (normally within two weeks) and by the division head for items over $100,000 (normally within three weeks). All design specifications must be approved by the EDP auditor (normally within four weeks).*

BUT:

ITEM	ACTION	BY	WEEKS
Design Specification	*Approve*	*EDP Auditor*	*4*
Package Design	*Review*	*Quality Assurance for compliance with standards*	*2*
Contract(s)	*Review*	*Law Department*	*3*
	Endorse	*DP Steering Committee*	*4*
Acquisition and Contract	*Approve*	*Under $100,000: Department head*	*2*
		Over $100,000: Division head	*3*

SENTENCES   Many factors contribute to readable sentences: choice of vocabulary, number of words in the sentence, sentence structure. The following hints can help you simplify your sentences.

Break a sentence joined by a semicolon or *and* into separate sentences.

NOT: *This long-range strategy report is presented in two parts; the first part deals with the five-year projections for computer usage and application requirements and the second part outlines our ten-year projections for these same items and also discusses industry trends and their possible*

> *impact on our decisions.*
>
> **BUT:** *This long-range strategy report has two parts. The first part presents five-year projections for computer usage and application requirements. The second part presents ten-year projections for these same items and also discusses industry trends and their possible impact on our decisions.*

Replace multiple items in a series with a bullet or numbered list. For example:

> **NOT:** *The programmer can insert into the code of the program commands to the precompilers to control the pagination of the listing of the program, blank lines between modules, the printing of titles and subtitles so that modules within the listing can easily be found, the ability to read alternate text files, and to turn the listing of parts of the program on or off.*
>
> **BUT:** *In the program code, you can insert commands to the precompilers to control:*
> - *Pagination of the program listing.*
> - *Blank lines between modules.*
> - *Printing titles and subtitles for modules.*
> - *Reading alternate text files.*
> - *Listing of parts of the program.*

Rephrase sentences containing such superfluous phrases as *There is (are), wherein, herein, whereas, that is (are),* and *which is (are).*

> **NOT:** *There are three conditions which must be met before continuing with the procedure.*
>
> **BUT:** *Three conditions must be met before continuing with the procedure.*

Eliminate parenthetical asides within a sentence. For example:

> **NOT:** *The XYZ terminal (now installed in the Boston, Atlanta, and Chicago offices) is replacing all terminals in company sales office.*
>
> **BUT:** *The XYZ terminal is replacing all terminals in company sales offices. The Boston, Atlanta, and Chicago offices have already installed XYZs.*

Cross out unnecessary words.

> **NOT:** *The data entry operator is the one who distributes reports.*
>
> **BUT:** *The data entry operator distributes reports.*

In the following sentences, brackets set off phrases that can be eliminated or simplified:

> *[The format of the] documentation [at this fourth level] should comply with the guidelines [on elements of documentation suitable] for [inclusion in one of the scientific and] technical publications [series with attendant review and editing procedures]. These programs should be documented [in a formal, rigorous manner,] with in-depth review [and special configuration control procedures enforced.]*

The sentences reduce to:

> *Level four documentation should comply with documentation*

℗ of Sandra Pakin & Associates, Inc.

> *guidelines for technical publications and must include in-depth review and editing.*

Change future tense (will) to present tense. For example:

> **NOT:** *The next screen will be the customer account screen.*
> **BUT:** *The next screen is the customer account screen.*

Use of future tense usually means you are writing from your own perspective. When the material is being read, it is now.

When you simplify your sentences, be sure you do not just make them short. You must also work to make them clearer. For example:

> **NOT:** *You need 14" by 11" continuous form paper which should be blank and you need a 10-pitch daisy wheel which should have the extended character set of 96 characters.*

and

> **NOT:** *You need 14" by 11" continuous form paper. The paper should be blank. You also need a 10-pitch daisy wheel. It should have the extended character set, which consists of 96 characters.*

> **BUT:** *You need blank 14" by 11" continuous form paper and a 10-pitch, 96-character daisy wheel.*

or

> **BUT:** *You need:*
> * *Blank 14" by 11" continuous form paper*
> * *10-pitch, 96-character daisy wheel*

LANGUAGE Most non-professional readers are comfortable reading at a tenth or eleventh grade level. Studies of reading comprehension have found that the number of syllables per word is one of three main factors in predicting reading ease. (The other factors are number of words per sentence and complexity of the sentence syntax.)

One way to make your materials easier to read is to use simple language when possible. For example:

> **NOT:** *Operating during prime computer time incurs substantially greater charges.*
> **BUT:** *Using computer services during the day from 8:00 a.m. to 5:00 p.m. costs more.*

Here are some other easy substitutions you can make:

NOT	BUT
utilization	*use*
in addition to	*besides*
facilitate	*help*
subsequent	*later*

Another way to simplify language is to write more precisely. For example:

NOT	BUT
The purpose of X is to provide	*X provides*
presents a summary of	*summarizes*
make a decision to	*decide*
take into consideration	*consider*
continues to remain	*remains*
The screen that is displayed first	*The first screen*
used for the purpose of	*used for*
in the event that	*if*

Style books are available that provide lists of these and similar terms. Appendix C, "Additional Reading on Writing Topics" lists several style books.

Avoid Patronizing and Overly Informal Language

In attempting to make a difficult subject palatable to readers, inexperienced writers often attempt to be too informal. The effect on readers is usually not positive. They are likely to feel that the writer is talking down to them or being patronizing. Your style should achieve a conversational tone without being chatty or slangy. For example:

NOT: *If all is okay, the whole mess is written to a TSO file.*
BUT: *If there are no errors, the data is written to a TSO file.*

NOT: *What else is special about the display screen? The "cursor" is! OK, already. What is a "cursor" and why do we need one?*
BUT: *A cursor is a special screen symbol that indicates where the next character you type will appear. It is either a blinking rectangle or underscore.*

NEVER: *If you've completed Step 341, you deserve a break. Go have a cup of coffee.*

It is your job as a writer to organize procedures, so none is so cumbersome as to require 341 steps. Do a better job of organizing and presenting the material.

Avoid Unnecessary Business and Computer Terminology

Computer-related documentation contains unavoidable business and computer terminology. However, writers insensitive to their audiences also use this terminology when it is not necessary. For example, it is not necessary to use the term *hardcopy* in a user's guide. *Report* is clearer for a user audience. Here are some easy substitutes you can make:

NOT	BUT
human resources	*people*
power on	*turn on*
hardware	*equipment*
software	*programs*
CPU	*computer*
input (verb)	*enter*

When computer terminology is necessary — because there is no everyday or simple substitute — you should explain the term the first time you use it and include it in the glossary.

In Conclusion

Although during rewrite you work to shorten sentences and paragraphs and eliminate unnecessary material, rewrite does not necessarily shorten your draft. Often during rewrite, you also:
- Clarify unclear or confusing statements.
- Add examples.
- Expand discussions.

These rewrite functions, while making your draft longer, help make it more understandable.

 ™ of Sandra Pakin & Associates, Inc.

Chapter 10

Preparing Reference Aids

Chapter 10
Preparing Reference Aids

How well readers accept a document depends on things the writer controls, such as:
- How the document looks.
- How easy it is to read.
- How easy the information is to find.

Format planning and graphic development account for the way the document looks. Outlining, writing, and rewriting account for how easy the document is to read. But another writer function — preparing reference aids — accounts for how easy the information is to find. This chapter concentrates on the preparation of four reference aids:
- Headings
- Tables of Contents
- Glossary
- Index

It also briefly discusses other specialized aids that help make documents more referenceable.

Headings

Headings or headlines introduce and highlight key points. They change the subject and signal the transition from topic to topic. Headings that reinforce and relate important information from the text increase the chances of the document's message getting across and being retained. By summarizing a topic, a heading alerts the interested reader to the supporting detail and permits the casual reader to find and skim the material. Without headings in the text, the reader has little idea what information is where, and he has to read the document as if it were a novel.

DEVELOPING HEADINGS

Heading development begins when you organize the information for your writing plan. Your topic outline represents a rough draft of your major headings.

Headings should take no more than half a line. The eye can grasp — and the brain interpret — a short title much faster than a long one that must be read with eye movement. But do not sacrifice clarity for brevity.

The heading must contain enough information to identify the topic content. Section, chapter, form, or report numbers should never serve as headings. They require the reader to memorize the order of the document or the codes for forms or reports.

At a chapter or major section level, one word may be sufficient to identify content — for example, "Recommendations." At a subject or topic level, several words may be required. Headings in the "Recommendations" section, for example, may be "Develop a Second Data Center," "Purchase Stand-alone Word Processing Equipment," and "Bring Timesharing Services In-house."

Often use of the rewriting principles can help with shortening or clarifying the heading. Eliminating unnecessary words makes headings shorter. With more precise language, headings are clearer. Some matching bad and improved examples of headings appear below:

NOT	**BUT**
A Guide to Using the Payroll System	*Using the Payroll System*
How to Code Input Forms	*Coding Input Forms*
Procedures for Updating the Master File	*Updating the Master File*
Understanding the File Structure	*File Structure*
Section One	*Purchase Stand-alone Word Processing Equipment*
Form RX271	*Order Ticket Form (RX271)*
Alternatives	*Data Base Design Alternatives*
Identification and Correction of Errors That Might Occur	*Troubleshooting*

CHECKING THE HEADINGS
The table of contents is a restatement of the headings within the text. Review the table of contents to verify that the reader can determine the content of each section from the heading he sees in the table of contents.

Tables of Contents

You need a table of contents for documents of more than 20 pages. Smaller documents such as reports and design presentations may require only a listing of the major sections. Manuals benefit from a table of contents that lists at least two levels of headings. If the manual is large enough to have divider tabs, include a chapter table of contents after each tab.

The headings and subheadings in the document form the basis for the table of contents. Two types of tables of contents are possible:
- Simple listing of headings and subheadings
- Annotated listing of headings and subheadings

SIMPLE LISTING
Your word processing operator can prepare the table of contents for you — if you provide instructions. He needs to know:
- Levels of headings to include and how to recognize them.
- Format for the table of contents.

™ of Sandra Pakin & Associates, Inc.

Levels of Headings

You may want to specify only two levels of headings for a manual table of contents, but include all headings in the chapter contents. The easiest way to identify the heading levels for your typist is to identify each heading in the text with a level number. Alternatively, you can give him a list of the heading formats. For example:

(1) <u>MAIN SECTION</u>   all caps and underscored

(2) SUBJECT   all caps

(3) <u>Topic</u>   Initial caps and underscored

Format for the
Tables of Contents

It is important that the reader see at a glance the relative importance of headings in the table of contents. Type or typing style and indenting can separate headings. The placement of the page numbers is also part of the format. Figure 10.1 shows different formats for a table of contents.

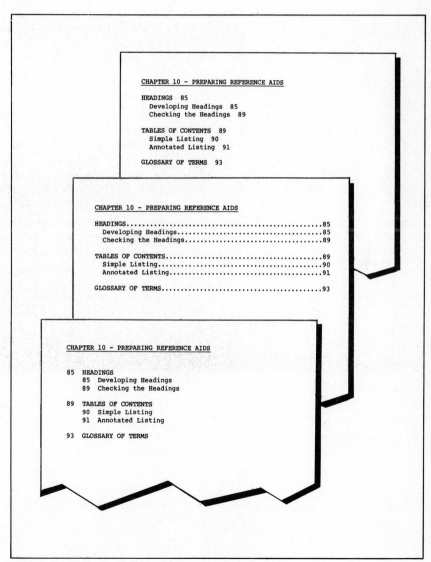

Figure 10.1 Formats for tables of contents

ANNOTATED LISTING

An annotated table of contents provides a summary statement of each section listed in the contents. Figure 10.2 shows an annotated table of contents used for a reports chapter.

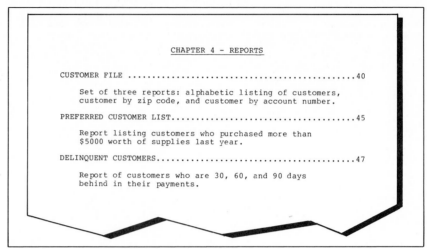

```
                    CHAPTER 4 - REPORTS

    CUSTOMER FILE ...........................................40

        Set of three reports: alphabetic listing of customers,
        customer by zip code, and customer by account number.

    PREFERRED CUSTOMER LIST.................................45

        Report listing customers who purchased more than
        $5000 worth of supplies last year.

    DELINQUENT CUSTOMERS....................................47

        Report of customers who are 30, 60, and 90 days
        behind in their payments.
```

Figure 10.2 Annotated table of contents

Glossary of Terms

A glossary — an alphabetic list of terms and their definitions — is an essential reference aid in user's and operator's guides. Unlike an index and a detailed table of contents, which help readers find information, the glossary makes it easy for readers to understand the information they read.

A good glossary helps create respect for your documentation and the system it supports, and it cuts down on readers' questions. The effectiveness of a glossary, however, depends on how well you understand the needs of the intended audience. Unless you have a clear notion of what the audience knows and does not know, you cannot make a glossary which serves your readers well.

Properly developed, a glossary gives readers quick access to definitions of all new terms and any that require special explanation in the context of the guide. For example, if the term *operator* means anyone who operates a terminal — including secretaries, professionals, and people with operator as their job title — the glossary should include this extended meaning of *operator*.

FINDING AND
SELECTING
GLOSSARY TERMS

Locating potential glossary items is a joint effort of writers and reviewers. You should begin to identify glossary items while the material is fresh — during planning and first draft writing. For each review draft and particularly on the first user review, ask reviewers to circle any new terms or unclear terms.

The following types of items may be suitable for the glossary in user's and operator's documents:
- Data processing terms
- Specialized business terms
- Application-specific terms
- Abbreviations

Data Processing Terms	Include data processing terms in the glossary, even common DP terms like *field, file, online, offline, disk, disk drive, tape drive, batch.* Also include data processing terms that are unique to the application or system — for example, *retention processing, dictionary member type, simulation mode.* However, it is not necessary to include specific names of reports and input forms, since these are best described in the text.
Specialized Business Terms	Terms used in a special way in your company or terms some readers may not recognize should be in the glossary. For example, *point-of-sale transaction, aged payable,* and *aged receivable* may mean something different in your company from their meaning in other businesses.
	A user's guide that assumes a level of business understanding and familiarity with business terms may not define these terms in the text. The glossary should define them. For example, a merchandise processing system manual might assume the primary reader knows merchandise processing terminology, such as *big ticket item, carrier,* and *drop-ship.* However, definitions of these terms in the glossary would aid other readers not familiar with them.
Application-Specific Terms	Some applications use terms and titles that have meaning only within the application. For example, an application may require altered or additional duties for a user and give that user an application-specific title. When an input coordinator, for instance, is responsible for collecting, checking, and submitting input forms for an application, *input coordinator* should be in the glossary.
Abbreviations	If the term is an abbreviation, no matter how common in your company, include it in the glossary and give its spelled out form as the definition. Then define the spelled out form as a separate glossary item.

WRITING GLOSSARY DEFINITIONS

Once you have identified the glossary terms, you are ready to define them. If you are going to alphabetize the terms manually, write the terms and their definitions on 3″ by 5″ index cards for easy sorting.

Figure 10.3 illustrates some of the characteristics of glossary definitions. A good glossary definition does not repeat the word it defines. It uses other words to describe the term simply and clearly. The definition itself immediately makes clear the part of speech (noun, verb, adjective) of the term being defined without using lead-in words such as *to, the, a,* or *an.*

Sources for Glossary Definitions	Your first source for glossary definitions is the text itself, since the text should explain terms the first time they are used. The definition in the glossary, however, should be more succinct and generally should not have supporting examples. Also, try not to use the exact words of the text so readers who do not understand the text have an alternate definition.

Some vendors have non-copyrighted glossaries of data processing terms which can provide glossary definitions — for example, *IBM Data Processing Glossary* (GC20-1699). In addition, the American National Standards Institute publishes the *American Dictionary for Information Processing* (1430 Broadway, New York, NY 10018).

When using these or other sources, you must write the definitions carefully so they reflect the way you actually use the term in the document. Standard definitions are often good guides, but they can seldom be adopted in full. For example, the following definition of *modem* is taken from the IBM glossary:

> **modem.** A functional unit that modulates and demodulates signals. One of the functions of a modem is to enable transmission of digital data over analog transmission facilities.

This definition is too technical for an operator's guide. A better definition would be:

> **modem.** Device that enables telephone lines to transmit computer data.

FORMATTING THE GLOSSARY

If your word processing equipment can produce boldface type, the glossary can be prepared with the term and definition in the same column, as shown with *modem*. To avoid type lines that are too long to be read easily, you can print two columns of terms on a page.

Figure 10.3 shows a two-column glossary format with terms in the narrower left column and definitions in the right column. This is a readable format for a typed glossary.

The terms in the figure are alphabetized in word-by-word order. This method groups all terms beginning with the same word. It contrasts with letter-by-letter alphabetizing, where word breaks are ignored and each letter is considered in the alphabetized arrangement. (In letter-by-letter alphabetizing, the first four terms in the figure would be *batch, data, database, data entry.)*

Except when the term itself is capitalized within the text, glossary items should be displayed in lower case. For single sentence definitions, begin the definition with a capital letter and end it with a period. If the definition requires multiple sentences, punctuate accordingly.

REVIEWING AND REVISING THE GLOSSARY

All regular reviewers of your user document should also review the glossary for accuracy, completeness, and clarity. To ensure that the glossary receives the attention it deserves, you may want to circulate just the glossary to knowledgeable reviewers. However, they should make their final review of the glossary in conjunction with the text. Be prepared to revise and add definitions based on the reviewers' comments.

Analytic Index

The index is a manual's key reference aid. Properly prepared, it gives your reader the means of quickly finding any item of detailed information.

An analytic index provides information to direct the reader to the discussion he needs. It requires specific details about various aspects of each topic. For example, compare the entries below:

> *variable, 20, 99, 116, 152*
>
> *variable*
> *contrasted with constant, 20*
> *global, 99*
> *label, 116*
> *list command, 152*
> *local, 99*
> *name, 20*

	batch	v) Collect input forms together as a set for key entry and processing.
		n) Collection of input forms treated as a set for key entry and processing.
	data	Information entered into the computer.
❷	data entry	Process of keying in and ensuring accuracy of information entered into the computer.
	database	Collection of information the system needs to perform its processing tasks.
❸	DDA	Demand Deposit Account.
	demand deposit account	Account from which a customer can make withdrawals by check.
	field	Space on an input form, screen, report, or file where a specific piece of information is entered, displayed, or stored.
	file update	Process of adding, changing, or deleting information on a file.
❹	key field	Unique field required to identify a record. Also called record ID. See field, required field.
❺	offline	Referring to procedures which are or can be performed without direct connection to the computer. Contrast with online.
❻	online	Referring to procedures which are performed on equipment connected to and directly controlled by the computer. Contrast with offline.
❼	record ID	Same as key field.
	required field	Input field that must be entered for the application to process.

❶ Verb definitions start with synonymous verbs. Most glossary items are nouns and their definitions being with synonymous nouns. It is not necessary, nor desirable, to begin definitions of verbs with *To* or definitions of nouns with *A, An,* or *The.*

❷ Since the glossary is not read consecutively, each glossary definition should be complete and not rely on a preceding definition for understanding.

❸ The glossary definition of an abbreviation is its spelled out version. Include a definition of the term under the spelled out version.

❹ If a term has a synonym that is also used, define the preferred term only and introduce the other term by *Also called.* If other terms in the glossary are related to this one, refer the reader to those terms using *See.*

❺ Adjective definitions are introduced by *Referring to, Pertaining to,* or *Having to do with.*

❻ If a term means the opposite of another term in the glossary (its antonym), introduce the antonym by *Contrast with.*

❼ If a term is not preferred, indicate the preferred glossary term by *Same as.* Include the definition only with the preferred term.

Figure 10.3 Glossary format

A list of page numbers following a general topic, as in the first example, does not help the reader pinpoint the discussion he needs. In the second example, the reader can tell exactly what aspect of the topic is discussed on each page.

Analytic indexing requires a knowledge of the manual, the purpose of the information, and the relationships among topics. Therefore, either the writer or the editor should select the index items.

Preparing an index involves the clerical processes of alphabetizing and formatting. If your department prepares several manuals a year, it would be valuable to have an indexing program. The processing requirements for the program would be to:

1. Alphabetize the input and print a listing to be used as a work copy.
2. Format the revised input into an index.

Some text processing systems have index capabilities. You identify each index item in the text with a special code for a main entry or a subentry, and the text processor alphabetizes and formats the index. Check with your text processing group to find out what indexing capabilities are available and how to use them.

STEPS IN PREPARING AN INDEX

Manual preparation of an analytic index requires four major steps:
- Finding the index items.
- Analyzing the items.
- Arranging the items.
- Formatting the items.

Finding the Index Items

For every 30-50 pages of text, you can easily prepare one double-column index page. Your manual is full of index items. You find them by reading the text and underlining or highlighting key words as potential index items. In your reading, be sure to identify key words in the section headings. Figure 10.4 is a composite of three pages with potential index items circled. Figure 10.6 shows part of the prepared index.

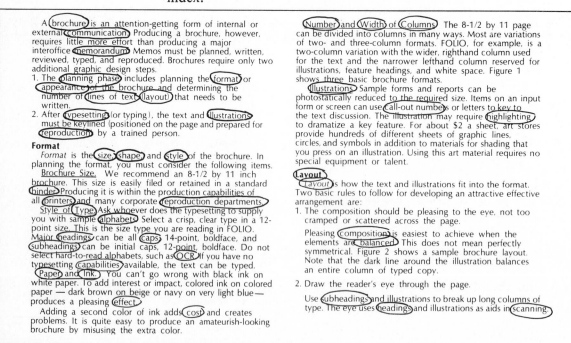

Figure 10.4 Circling the potential index items in the text

™ of Sandra Pakin & Associates, Inc.

Analyzing the Items

Think about the highlighted words as you go through the text a second time. Are they important to the subject? Are they understandable? *Form, appearance, steps,* and *capabilities* are too general. Modify general terms — for example, *graphic design steps, production capabilities.* Should any highlighted words be subitems under a more general topic?

Write each potential index topic on a separate 3″ by 5″ card, along with any associated subitem information and the page number. Cards are used to make alphabetizing and rearranging items easier. One key word may require several cards, as shown in Figure 10.5.

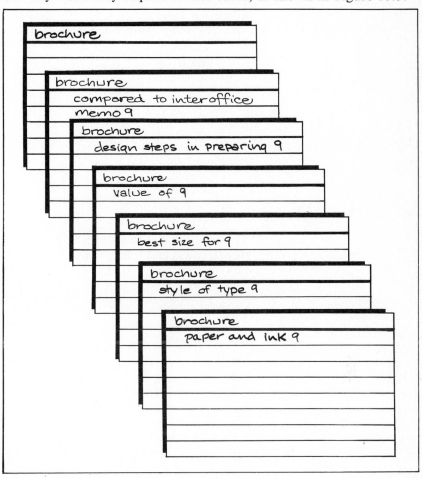

Figure 10.5 Using cards to record index items

Arranging the Items

Alphabetize your cards first by the main topic and then alphabetize within subitems. The cards of Figure 10.5 for the index item *brochure* are arranged: brochure; brochure, best size for; brochure, compared to interoffice memo; brochure, design steps in preparing; brochure, paper and ink; brochure, style of type; brochure, value of.

Then read the cards. Items or subitems may be the same or similar and should be combined into one item with multiple page numbers. You may not know what you meant by a particular entry. Go back to the page and find a better way of saying what you intended.

Formatting the Index

Have the index typed in index format. Figure 10.6 shows part of the index created from Figure 10.4. Note the indenting for the subitems.

art materials
    for creating brochure illustrations, 10
balance, 10
boards, 11
brochure
    best size for, 9
    compared to interoffice memo, 9
    format, 9
    layout, 10
    paper and ink, 9
    steps, in preparing, 9
    style of type, 9
    value of, 9
call out numbers
    used to key illustrations to text, 10
columns
    number of, 10
    width of, 10
composition, 10
cost
    of adding additional color ink, 10
    of producing a brochure, 9

format, 9
galley, 11
graphic design
    steps in preparing a brochure, 9
headings
    aid in scanning, 10
illustration
    for a brochure, 10
    placement on page, 11
ink
    adding a second color, 10
    color for a brochure, 9
keylining, 9
layout, 10
memorandum
    steps in preparing, 9
OCR
    avoid using this alphabet, 9
paper
    kind for a brochure, 9
paste-up, 11

Figure 10.6 *Analytic index*

Specialized Aids

Three additional reference aids regularly used in manuals are tabs, page headers and footers, and illustration lists. These are discussed in this section.

TABS If a document has major sections, it should use tabs. Tabs can be blind tabs or divider tabs. A blind tab is a black semi-circle printed at the outer edge of the first page of a section or chapter so that a dark line shows when you look at the side of the manual. Another form of blind tab is a colored page inserted before each major section or chapter.

Blind tabs are inexpensive to produce and require no special binding. The disadvantage to a blind tab is that it includes no section or chapter title.

Divider tabs are heavy paper with a protruding tab on which you can write the section or chapter title. Always print the chapter title on both sides of the tab. You diminish the benefit of the divider tab for reference if you print chapter numbers or letters on the tab instead of the chapter title.

Divider tabs provide excellent referenceability. However, they require a binding where the covers of the binder extend beyond the tabs to prevent them from bending. Divider tabs are also relatively expensive.

HEADERS AND FOOTERS Page headers and footers make it easier to page through the document. The following information in the header or footer helps the reader find information:

- Page number
- Chapter title
- Subject title

Page numbers should be placed on the outside portion of the page.

For two-sided printing, the page number of lefthand pages is at the left and at the right for righthand pages. For one-sided printing, the page number is at the right.

ILLUSTRATION LIST   Particularly in manuals where figures provide additional information, an illustration list can be a helpful reference aid. Include an illustration list, for example, when figures show samples of reports, screens, and forms.

Positioned immediately after the manual table of contents, the illustration list contains:
- Figure number
- Caption or other identification, such as table name
- Page number

Arrangement of the Document's Components

Preparation of the document's reference aids completes the text portion of the manual. After adding graphics, assemble a manual in the following order:

FRONT MATTER
Title page
Preface
Manual table of contents
Illustration list

FOR EACH CHAPTER
Chapter tab
Chapter table of contents
Chapter text

BACK MATTER
Appendix tab
Appendixes
Glossary tab
Glossary
Index tab
Index
Reader's comment form

Alternatively, the back matter can have one tab, labeled Reference.

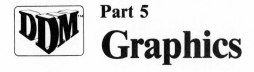 **Part 5**

Graphics

Well-planned page formats, illustrations, and figures help alleviate boredom and increase the communicative quality of MIS documents.

One of the goals of the Documentation Development Methodology is to improve the readability of MIS documents through effective format planning and the use of reader-directed graphics and illustrations.

Illustrations eliminate the need for extensive narrative explanations of visual information. An illustration of a control panel, for instance, clarifies an operating procedure. For discussions involving input documents, reports, or display screens, examples make the discussion easier to follow.

Graphic skills are necessary for the following tasks:
- Task 1 - Plan Documentation Project
- Task 3 - Plan Document Format
- Task 6 - Develop Graphics
- Task 8 - Rewrite and Complete Graphics

Chapters 11, 12, and 13 discuss the graphics activities needed to complete these tasks.

Chapter 11 - Page Format and Layout

The basic page format for all documents in the project is determined during project planning. During document planning, you adapt the page format to the specific document. Finally, during document development, the format becomes the structure for the arrangement of text and illustrations on the page. This arrangement is the page layout. This chapter discusses the techniques for creating the page format and layout.

Chapter 12 - Format Standards

During project planning, you determine the format standards for the documentation project. This chapter explains how to formulate the text and graphic format standards.

Chapter 13 - Graphic Development

With readily available supplies and illustration sources like report printouts and photographs, your department can create most graphics for MIS materials. This chapter explains several ways you can develop graphics for your document. It also discusses how to work with a graphic artist.

Chapter 11
Page Format and Layout

Chapter 11

Page Format and Layout

The way a document looks is important. Disorganized placement of elements on a page distracts readers, and too much uninterrupted text bores some readers. But a well-planned, graphically interesting document attracts readers and holds their attention.

Decisions on page format and writing and graphic standards take place during format planning. Company standards, the project's presentation requirements, and knowledge of some basic techniques influence these decisions. Within the established standards, the graphic needs of the individual document determine the actual page layout. This chapter discusses and illustrates format and layout techniques.

Determining Page Format

The format of the page is the basic structure for the placement of all text and graphics. It is not a page layout, which is the actual arrangement of specific text and illustrations on a given page.

During format planning, you determine such interrelated elements as:

- Placement of text and headings on the page
- Margins
- Positions for control information such as manual name, page number, and publication date

TEXT AND HEADING PLACEMENT

To determine the placement of the text and headings, you need to define the number of columns of text. For typed copy, this should be within the capabilities of your word processing equipment and should not place an unusual burden on your typist. Heading placement depends upon the column decision. The format of this book, for example, uses a modified two-column format with only headings in the left column. Publications using a single wide column of text or two columns of equal size usually put the headings within the text column.

MARGINS

Before determining margins, you must know the page size, kind of binding to be used, and placement of text and headings. Then you can decide upon a margin size to support these decisions. Use the following procedure as a guide to determining your document's margins.

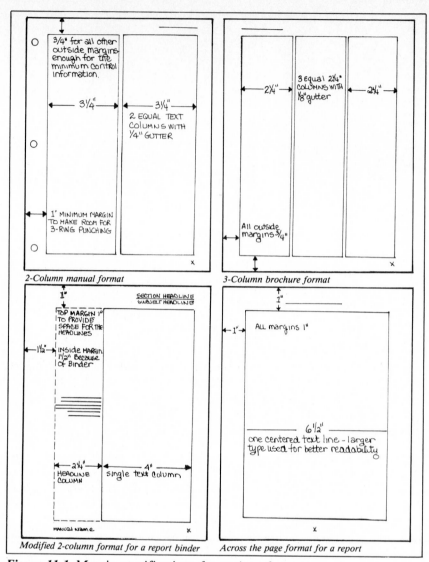

Figure 11.1 *Margin specifications for various formats*

1. Determine minimum margins.
   - The kind of binding and printing determines minimum left and right margins. For example, a heat-sealed binding needs extra wide inner margins so the text is not lost in the curl of the open book. For one-sided printing to go into a three-ring binder, a wider left margin is needed to clear the holes.
   - The amount of and spacing for control information determine the minimum top and bottom margins.
2. Determine line length. For ease in scanning the text line, the line length should be between four and six inches. This is between 48 and 64 characters of 12-pitch typing or between 40 and 60 characters of 10-pitch typing. If you planned on a single-column of text and the minimum margins allow too wide a space for text, widen the left and right margins or use a two-column format.

™ of Sandra Pakin & Associates, Inc.

3. Prepare a mockup page, demonstrating your placements and margin decisions. Do you like it? Does it allow enough white space to make the page inviting? Adjust your placement and margin decisions within the minimum margin constraints until you are satisfied.

Figure 11.1 shows four format variations and the margin specifications for each.

CONTROL INFORMATION

Control information helps a reader locate and identify pages. Before you can determine the placement of control information on a page, you must decide what control information you need. At a minimum, control information should include:

- Document identification
- Page number

Additionally, you may want to include one or more of the following:

- Publication or revision date. Useful when many updates will be incorporated into a manual over its lifetime.
- Corporate logo. Identifies the ownership of the material.
- Software product logo. Identifies the software product family this document belongs to.
- Section and subject title headers or footers. Adds to the referenceability of manuals and long reports.
- Word processing document number. Aids in finding the document or file in the word processing system.

Select only enough control information to serve your referencing, documentation control, and update needs.

Figure 11.2 illustrates two variations in the placement of control information for manuals.

Placing the control information on the page is a matter of balance

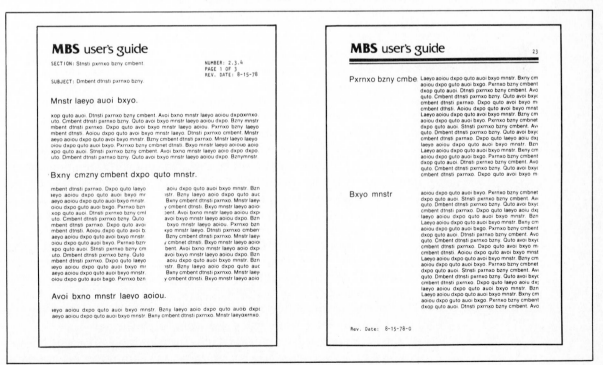

Figure 11.2 Placement of control information

™ of Sandra Pakin & Associates, Inc.

and preference. Control information is generally as small and unobtrusive as possible. Control information in this book, for example, is slightly outside the page margin area, to set it apart from the text. The book logo is in the upper inside corners. The chapter title is in the upper left corner of even-numbered pages, and the section title is in the upper right corner of odd-numbered pages. Page numbers are in the lower outside corners.

Specifying Page Layout

The page format is the structure for unchanging elements on all pages of all documents associated with the project. The arrangement of the text, headings, and graphics on a *specific* page is the layout of that page. When you prepare sample pages during document planning, you are demonstrating typical page layouts for the document.

Although the page format provides structure and continuity for the appearance of the document or documents in the project, it is not a cast-iron mold that eliminates any graphic creativity. An effective layout works within the page format to make the best visual presentation for the document's audience. Use these two guidelines for your layout decisions:

- Keep the layout simple.
- Suit the layout to the purpose.

KEEP LAYOUT SIMPLE
Unless you have professional production support for layout and final preparation of the pages, avoid layouts that require special page preparation or variations in line length. For example, magazines often wrap columns of text around an illustration or photograph. This can be an effective layout, but it requires extra text planning and special preparation. Therefore, this type of layout is not suitable for documents produced without graphic support.

Figure 11.3 shows two layouts easily produced without graphic support.

SUIT LAYOUT TO THE PURPOSE
The first thing a reader sees about your document is the way the pages look, and the appearance affects whether he reads the material. Pages crammed top to bottom with unrelieved text discourage some readers. If the pages look too simple, others may think your document lacks substance. The text and illustrations must be positioned to suit the purpose of the document.

A report that presents the decision framework of a long-range strategy, for example, has a great deal of supporting technical detail. The report's readers want to know not only the conclusions but also all the facts that support the conclusions. For this kind of document, the need for detail governs the nature and arrangement of text and illustrations.

If the material being presented is procedural, readers want to read only what they must do to carry out the procedure. Long or complex discussions do not attract them. They appreciate a high illustrations-to-text ratio.

Layout Examples
The following discussion and figures illustrate how material can be laid out differently while using the same page format.

The page format in Figure 11.4 positions control information and establishes a line length and margins to guarantee a *minimum* amount of white space on the page. The page format margins in-

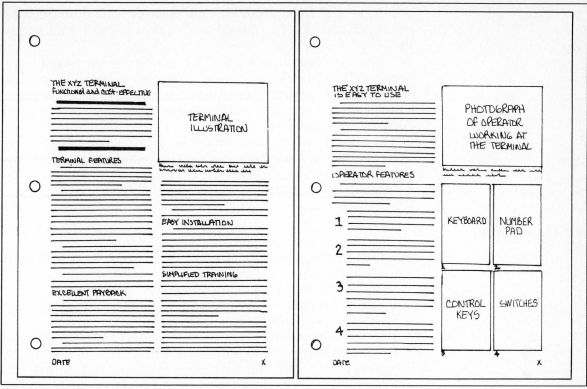

Figure 11.3 *Two layouts for opening page of a section. Each adapts the format for a different purpose and audience.*

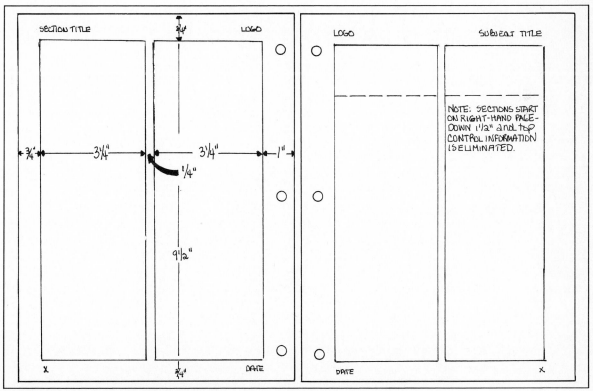

Figure 11.4 *Page format for a project*

dicate where text *cannot* go. But having margins established does not mean that every inch of the space within the margins must be used up.

The writer's layouts in Figure 11.4 use the format established in Figure 11.3 for the first page of a section. Each discusses the same terminal. Each, however, alters the arrangement of the information and the number and type of illustrations to suit the purpose of the document being written.

The layout for the management guide provides more copy with an overview summary, good headlines, and a single diagram. The layout for the data entry guide limits the amount of copy and uses several photographs to clearly show the terminal features.

In Conclusion

The page format gives all documents within a series continuity by uniformly treating:
- Width and placement of text columns
- Size of margins
- Position of control information

Within the format, the writer exercises creativity to arrange such elements as headings, text, and illustrations. Although layouts may vary from page to page, similar content should be laid out similarly. For example, all screen illustrations and descriptions should have the same layout.

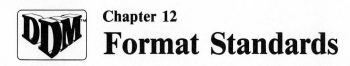 **Chapter 12**
Format Standards

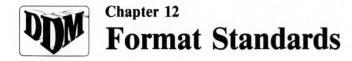

Chapter 12

Format Standards

You begin defining text and graphic format standards during project planning. Then as you plan and develop the first document, you refine the format standards. Format standards are part of the project writing guide.

Text Format Standards

Text standards specify how headings and text are typed or typeset. They also cover punctuation, capitalization, and spelling style. Typing instructions are based on text format standards.

HEADING STANDARDS   Headings should stand out from the text. The spacing around the headings and the way they are typed makes them prominent.

Vertical spacing before and after the heading sets off the heading. All headings should be typographically distinguishable from the text to ensure that even the cursory reader notices them. In typeset copy, for example, some headings can be in boldface type to set them off, as in this book.

When you are using a word processing system, use all the facilities of your system to make the headings stand out. For typewritten documents, combinations of underscoring and upper- and lower-case letters can suggest the weight or level of detail of the headings, as shown below.

<u>MAJOR SECTION TITLE</u>

SUBSECTION TITLE

<u>Topic Title</u>

<u>Run-in Paragraph Title</u>. The text continues on the same line as the heading.

A numbering hierarchy can indicate a heading's level of detail:

1.   <u>MAJOR SECTION TITLE</u>

1.1   SUBSECTION TITLE

1.1.1 <u>Topic Title</u>

Numbering every heading level is unnecessary. This method becomes cumbersome for more than three levels — for example, a fourth level sub-heading would be 2.4.3.1. Major section and subsection headings can be numbered, and typographical variations can differentiate the remaining topics.

SPACING STANDARDS Developing spacing standards for your text is relatively simple. It is a matter of specifying how spacing — both vertical and horizontal — is going to be used to improve the readability and appearance of the text. For instance, typed text is easier to read when spaces differentiate paragraphs. Therefore, single-spaced text with an extra line between paragraphs is easier to read than straight single-spaced or double-spaced text. Some studies also indicate that indented paragraphs increase text readability.

Besides the decision to double-space between paragraphs, you must establish spacing standards for the following:

Vertical Spacing
- Before and after figures and examples.
- Between items in a list.
- Before and after headings. Does the spacing vary with the level of heading?

Horizontal Spacing
- Number of spaces, if any, to indent for paragraphs.
- Number of spaces, if any, to indent for bullet and numbered lists.
- Number of spaces between the bullet or number and text in a list.
- Placement of headings — centered, or starting or ending at a margin.
- Placement of figure captions — centered, or starting at the left edge of the figure.

TYPE STANDARDS For typed documents, few type variations are available — usually type size of 10- or 12-pitch and perhaps italics. Since changing type elements on most word processing systems is cumbersome and time-consuming, the type is usually limited to one type style and size per document. But typesetting and some word processing systems have great flexibility in type size, style, and intensity.

Some readability studies indicate that serif type improves text readability. Serif type (as shown in Figure 12.1) has little lines at the top and bottom of each letter. The opposite is sans serif type which does not have these lines (or serifs). For typing, letter gothic is a common sans serif type style, and courier is a common serif style.

serif sans serif

Figure 12.1 Serif and sans serif type

™ of Sandra Pakin & Associates, Inc.

When type variation is available, headings can receive special type treatment. You may want to consider the following options when determining standards:

- Producing all figure captions and examples in a smaller type size. Italic type is often used to differentiate between the main portion of the text and figure captions.
- Using italic type for anything underlined in a typewritten text, such as book titles and new vocabulary words that require special emphasis.
- Distinguishing summary or particularly important statements with a special type style. Boldface type, for example, highlights a special caution.

Variations in type must be handled with caution. Too many different type elements on a page are distracting.

If you plan to have your document typeset or produced on a word processing system with type variations, seek an expert's help in establishing the type standards. A word processing supervisor or typesetter can give you suggestions for type standards and guidelines for marking up your copy to be sure you maintain these standards.

Graphic Format Standards

Just as you lay out the page to attract the intended audience, you select a graphic style that also fits that audience. Highly detailed drawings required by a technical audience, for example, may be unnecessarily complex for a user's guide.

DETERMINING
GRAPHIC APPROACH

To determine the graphic approach for your document, first analyze your audience, then consider these additional factors:

- Tone and language style of the text. A formal presentation requires more formal illustrations.
- Types of illustrations. If most of your illustrations are reports and screen representations, drawings may be out of place.
- Available graphic support and reproduction facilities. You have to work within your resources and budget in determining your graphic approach.

As an illustration of how a graphic approach varies, consider the processing flow, a standard illustration that appears in many types of documents. Flows can, for example, demonstrate how information moves through an application, how materials arrive at a production point, or how work is apportioned to various employees. Flows can be prepared in many different ways to suit the audience of the document.

The flow shown in Figure 12.2 is a standard processing flow developed by an MIS professional. Technical MIS audiences have no trouble understanding this kind of flow in programming documentation and technical reports.

A common mistake in documents directed to non-technical audiences is the use of illustrations prepared for a technical audience. Illustrations must change to suit the needs and interest level of the intended reader. For example, you can simplify and change the flow of Figure 12.2 to suit any audience and presentation. Figure 12.3 shows a typed format for the flow appropriate for a management overview. Figure 12.4 demonstrates two other graphic approaches to the same material.

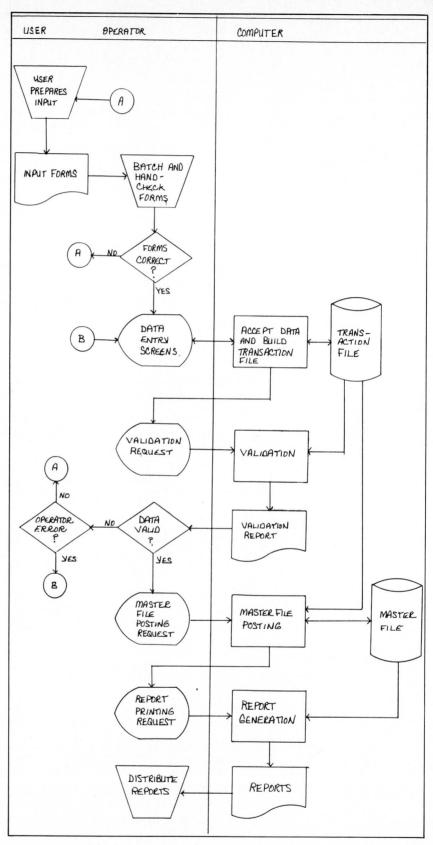

Figure 12.2 Technical processing flow

PROCESSING FLOW

 PLANNING

1. Assemble user-prepared input forms in batches

2. Assign batch number and maintain batch control.

3. Manually check each batch for missing information. Return forms with missing *required* information to the user.

 DATA ENTRY

4. Enter data onto the system.

5. Validate entered data. Correct entry errors, return input form errors to the user.

6. Update the masterfile with the corrected information.

REPORTING

7. Initiate report printing.

8. Receive and distribute reports.

Figure 12.3 Typed processing flow

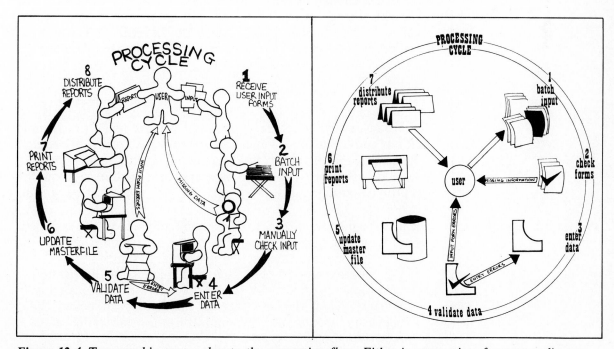

Figure 12.4 Two graphic approaches to the processing flow. Either is appropriate for user audiences.

PRESENTING FIGURES Graphic standards deal with style of the graphics, the way they appear in the text. All figures of the same type should be shown the same size, have information identified on them in the same way, and be similarly captioned and referred to from the text. Therefore, most of the graphic standards you specify concern the way figures are presented, including:

- Presentation style
- Illustration explanations
- Information identification

Presentation Style The first step in developing the presentation style is to determine the kinds of graphics to be included in the document — input forms, CRT screens, reports, equipment photographs or diagrams, processing flows. Once you have identified the graphic categories, you can determine the standards for each type to ensure a uniform presentation style.

To demonstrate, consider the development of standards for report printouts. All report printouts should be handled in the same way in the text. This means uniform standards for size, callouts, highlighting, and percent of reduction. For report detail to be readable, for example, you should never reduce the report more than 50%. In addition, you should determine whether the report is:

- Shown alone or related to the input form(s).
- Boxed in and shown with pinfeed holes.
- Shown completely or in part.

When only a small portion of the information on a report is pertinent, you can reduce the entire report more than 50%, but present the pertinent information in larger detail, as shown in Figure 12.5.

Chapter 13, "Graphic Development," presents a variety of ways to prepare standard graphic elements.

Reproduction Preparation. Most computer printers do not produce a clear enough image once the report is reduced and duplicated on the document page. Therefore, during planning, you should check to see how reports reproduce at the reduction you have specified. Additionally, to improve readability, change the ribbon on the printer and use plain white paper.

If the best report printout simply is not readable, consider typing the report. A typist can probably type all the report examples in your document in one or two days. (Because of likely system changes, you should not undertake report typing until you are ready to assemble field test copy. For the technical review copy, use report printouts.)

Remember that if reports need typing and special reductions, you must add sufficient time to the development schedule to allow for this production step. Also, if reports are typed, they must be carefully proofread.

Illustration Explanations The text should always refer to or explain figures. How this is done is part of your standards and may depend on the type of figure or the way your text handles figures. Three possibilities are:

- Figures may support text discussion, such as the illustration of a report printout with report columns being discussed in the text. Then the reference to the figure can be an explanatory note in the text indicating location rather than figure number. For example:

The system planning report, shown above, provides fifteen types

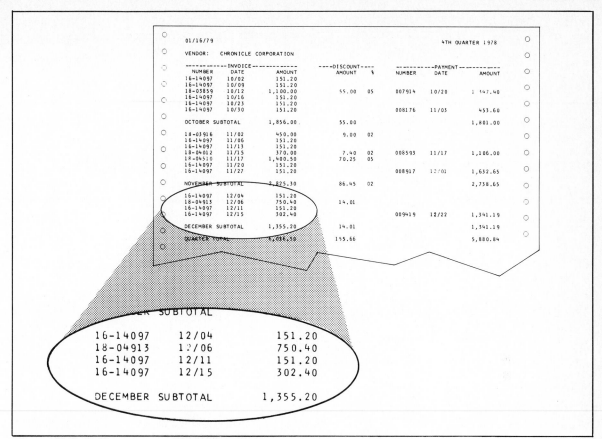

Figure 12.5 Calling out specific information

of specialized planning information. The discussion provides an explanation of each of the fields in the order it appears on the report. For reference, the field discussions are numbered to correspond with the identifying numbers on the example report.

* Figures may provide additional information not supplied in the text. This information can be provided as part of the figure as in Figure 12.8 or in a figure caption. The text referring to the figure should indicate the type of information it provides. For example:

    Figure 16 shows how you enter information from the purchase order into the order entry system.

* Figures may simply provide an appropriate illustration for the discussion in the text. For example:

    The XYZ terminal, illustrated on this page, has several highly efficient operator features.

Information Identification Sometimes the detail in a figure can be overwhelming for the reader unless he receives some help in finding the information. In other cases, the reader needs to know the significance of what he is seeing. Callouts are one method of helping the reader. Figure 12.6 shows how verbal callouts highlight the word processing format features being shown in the illustration.

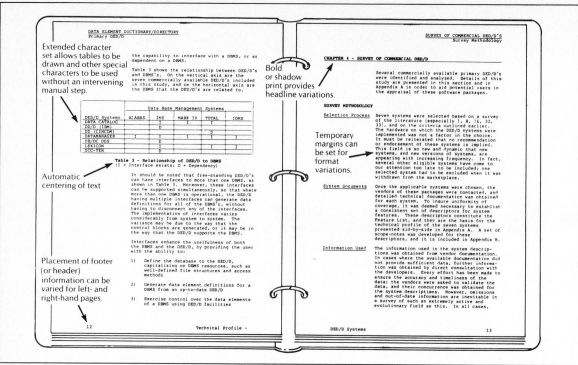

Figure 12.6 Verbal callout of features

If you want to include a text explanation to correspond to the items on the figure, you can use numbers or letters to call out information. Your standards must establish the rules for all graphic devices, including callouts. When developing standards for number or letter callouts, follow these rules:

- Arrange callouts in a logical, easy-to-follow order.
- Introduce text discussion with a similar graphic. Figure 10.3 is an example of how to do this.
- Do not call out more information than you can discuss on the same page (or a facing page for front/back reproductions). Repeat the figure on the new page and call out just the information discussed on that page.
- Style, size, and format of callouts should be consistent throughout the document.

Figure 12.7 shows two types of callouts.

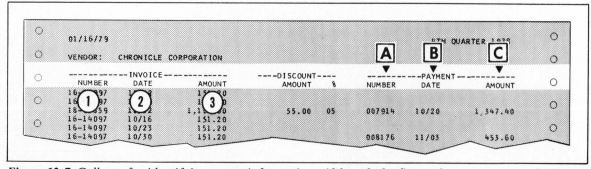

Figure 12.7 Callouts for identifying report information. Although the figure shows two types of callouts, select only one type as your standard.

148

PROVIDING DATA
IN FIGURES

As computer systems become more complex, it becomes more difficult to explain them to users. System prototypes, report mockups, and simulated screens help the user visualize a proposed system. One way to improve the effectiveness of screen and report illustrations in manuals is to show them with data. If data-filled examples are a standard for your documents, you must determine the source of the data. This might be:

- System test or user acceptance test data.
- Data made up for each example.
- Case study data (as in Figure 12.8).

The first two sources are common and do not need explanation. A case study establishes an operating scenario that reflects the user's processing needs. It sets up a sample processing environment so data on input forms and entry screens and the information on sample reports are related and easy for the user to understand.

As shown in Figure 12.8, when you use a case study, the data on

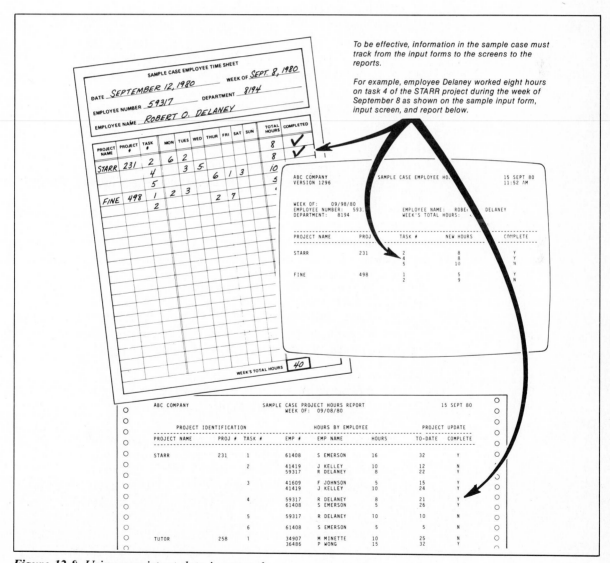

Figure 12.8 *Using consistent data in examples*

sample input documents matches data entered on sample screens and then is reflected in information on reports.

Besides providing data for consistent examples in user and operator documentation, a case study can also be a tutorial for training or can sell the system to new or potential users.

Checklist for Project Writing Guide

Although specifying format standards is a detailed job, it need be done only once for a project. After you have determined the text and graphic format standards, collect them in the project writing guide. The following checklist presents standards to consider for your project writing guide. Appendix B shows the project writing guide for this book.

PAGE FORMAT
- [ ] Text. What type style is used? What pitch? What line length? What margins?
- [ ] Pagination: How many lines per page?
- [ ] Line spacing. Between paragraphs? Between sections?
- [ ] Page numbering. Are pages numbered within section, within chapter, or consecutively throughout the document?
- [ ] Header and footer. Content? How close to the top of the page is the header printed? How many line spaces separate the header from the text? How many line spaces separate the text from the footer?

HEADINGS
- [ ] How are the various levels of headings indicated? Where do they appear on the page? How do they appear in the table of contents?

LISTS
- [ ] Where are the bullets or numbers placed? How many spaces before the text begins? Are list items doublespaced or singlespaced? How are lists to be punctuated?

PUNCTUATION
- [ ] How are dashes represented? Can words be hyphenated? How are you going to capitalize form, report, and screen names, system messages, and the names of keys?

FIGURES
- [ ] Captions. How are figures numbered? How are captions treated when the same figure is repeated on subsequent pages?
- [ ] Spacing. How many spaces between the figure number and caption? How many line spaces before and after figures and what spacing between the figure and the caption?
- [ ] Presentation. What should be capitalized? What typography should be used? What are the standard figure sizes? Are figures boxed?
- [ ] Textual references. How are figures to be identified in the text?

ARTWORK SPECIFICATIONS

- ☐ Types of illustrations.
- ☐ Callouts and shading. What materials are used? Provide descriptions and order numbers.
- ☐ Reductions. What percent reduction is used for forms, screens, and reports?
- ☐ Specific instructions. As artwork is developed, notes should be added to the project writing guide on such matters as sources and special materials.

TABLES

- ☐ How are the column headings capitalized?
- ☐ What should be done when a table continues to a second page?
- ☐ Where is the table title placed?

WORD LIST

- ☐ What are the special terms and spellings? List all that might cause problems. For example, most banks spell *installment* with only one "l," *instalment*.
- ☐ What are the standard dictionary and data processing glossary?

SUPPORT SERVICES

- ☐ Who by function and department is responsible for word processing, reproduction, graphic arts, binders, tabs, paper?
- ☐ What instructions should be given to support services?

REFERENCES

- ☐ What style guide should be referred to for questions not answered by the project writing guide?
- ☐ What dictionary should be used for spelling?
- ☐ What data processing glossary should be used for data processing terms?

® of Sandra Pakin & Associates, Inc.

Graphic Development

Chapter 13
Graphic Development

You have three basic sources for illustrative materials for your documents. You can:
- Create the figures within your department, with someone in your department doing all development.
- Use available illustrations or photographs and prepare them within your department or with the help of some external support service.
- Work with a graphic artist who handles all preparation to your specifications.

This chapter discusses how to use each of these sources.

Creating Figures within Your Department

The first step in developing graphics within your MIS department is understanding what materials and supplies are available to simplify this task. The second step is having someone in your department learn to use the supplies.

It is generally cost-effective to assign one person to the graphic preparation tasks for all documents, because he develops his skills by doing the required tasks. Pasting illustrations into place on text pages, for example, is a skill that requires the ability to line things up properly and check or measure for proper placement. With practice, tasks like applying callouts and pasting down illustrations become simple and quick.

SHOPPING FOR SUPPLIES

If your department provides graphic support for documents, you can get more professional-looking results by using some basic graphic supplies.

For example, suppose the text shows a 14" by 11" computer-printed report and describes how to read it. You can use press-down callout numbers to identify columns, templates to add arrows, and shading film to create special emphasis.

Use tape or correcting fluid to mask unwanted marks or portions of the report. Then reduce the report and paste it onto the page. Finally, using a good black pen and ruler, draw a box around the entire report. The result is a graphically appealing exhibit in your manual.

The supplies you need for graphic support can be found at a well-equipped stationery store or, preferably, at an art supply store. The items in the shopping list are the graphic supplies needed to create, correct, position, and paste down figures.

Creating Exhibits To develop figures and illustrations or to provide graphic emphasis in the text, use these simple tools.

- Black pens. Use black marking pens with tips of various widths to draw lines, fill in areas, print letters, make minor art corrections, and draw designs with templates.
- Templates. Templates are available with symbols for almost every business specialty and with various sizes of geometric shapes, arrows, brackets, and small designs. You follow the shape, using a fine point pen, to draw consistent designs or symbols or create illustrations.
- Ruler. Use a metal-edged ruler to draw fine, straight lines and measure accurately. Another useful ruler is one that gives characters per inch and lines per inch.
- Press-down illustrations and letters. Press-down art is available in hundreds of letter designs and sizes, symbols, art designs, and dot patterns (screens). Screens are especially useful for highlighting sections of a figure. Callout numbers or letters, arrows, brackets, or lines can be used to identify parts of a figure or text.
- Burnishing tool. Use a burnishing tool to make press-down art adhere permanently to the page. Although anything with a smooth hard surface works, the burnishing tool is designed for this task.
- Tracing vellum. Tracing vellum is a non-porous paper for developing forms or doing original art work. The paper has no irregularities to reproduce on the copies. Press-art or letters go on uniformly and ink from marking pens does not bleed as it is absorbed. Tracing vellum is also available with non-reproducible blue lines to serve as a guide in the placement of art and captions.

Making Corrections In the development of illustrations, corrections and deletions are inevitable. Various graphic tools can help.

- White-out tape. Special white tape, available in a variety of widths, can cover seams or smooth edges when pasting on art or corrections. The tape helps eliminate shadows that can result from adding layers of paper. You can also use the white-out tape to cover items that you wish to delete. If white-out tape is not available, gummed labels also work.
- White-out fluid. Typing correction fluid cleans up small marks on a page and corrects art work. The correction fluid developed especially for photo-reproduced copies should always be used when the figure is a copy.
- Gum eraser. A gum eraser removes slight excesses of glue or smudges on a page. It erases pencil marks, dirt, and rubber cement and does not leave smudges or tear the paper.
- Razor knife. The razor knife is a sharp blade in a special handle. It is useful for trimming press-down shading and cutting out small areas from text or art. It is easy to control and the blades come in a variety of points and edges.

Positioning the Artwork When you prepare artwork for pasting onto the text page, you need to size and identify it for its proper position on the appropriate page. The following tools are helpful.

- Reducing wheel. The reducing wheel, shown in Figure 13.1, is

156

a scale for determining proportions and percents for reductions and blowups of illustrations. It can determine either the percent of change needed to reach a certain size or the size that will result from a certain percent of change.

- Non-repro pen or pencil. Since certain colors, primarily light blues, do not photo-reproduce, you can use this type of pen or pencil to mark on the finished copy or art. This is especially useful when marking the page for positioning of artwork or making corrections for a typist. However, some copiers pick up the non-repro colors. Be sure your copier drops out the non-repro colors before using them to mark originals or pages ready for production.

- Grease pencil or soft lead pencil. Mark artwork or illustrations on the back with a grease pencil or a very soft lead pencil. Hard pencils or pens make an indentation that is visible from the front, and felt tip markers can bleed through.

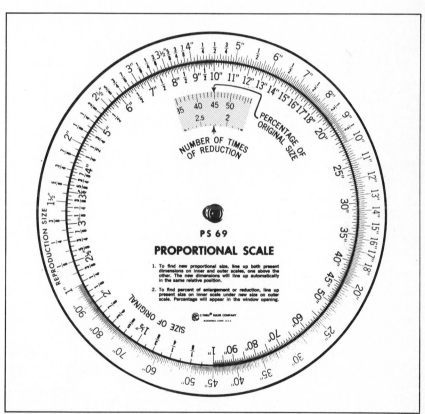

Figure 13.1 Reducing wheel. Instructions for using the wheel are usually printed on it.

Pasting Down the Art   Adhesive or tape is used to affix the finished art to the text page, depending on the type of bond required.

- Transparent tape. For review copies, use transparent tape. If put on smoothly and pressed down, it creates very little shadow or tone difference in the reproduction copy.

- Spray adhesive. Spray adhesive is indispensable for pasting down large illustrations or blocks of copy. There are two kinds of spray adhesive — one for immediate permanent bonding and one for temporary mounts. For most uses, the temporary mount is better because the figure can be repositioned. After a time, the mount becomes permanent.

- Rubber cement. With very small pieces of art or copy, the spray adhesive may be difficult to control. In these cases, use one-coat rubber cement. The material can be repositioned. After a time, the mount becomes permanent.

Graphic artists usually use wax as an adhesive. Wax-coated material adheres well, can be repositioned, and never becomes permanently bonded. Wax coaters, however, are expensive.

The key to the effectiveness of all purchased materials is learning to use them. The next two sections suggest simple ways someone in your department can use standard art materials to prepare illustrations for your documents. Your art supplier can provide you with additional instructions and suggestions on positioning artwork and using various graphic tools and supplies.

USING TEMPLATES TO
DEVELOP GRAPHICS

Most graphics used in MIS documents do not have to be realistic or detailed illustrations. They need only suggest objects or concepts. This section illustrates and discusses how to use templates to create seven widely used data processing graphics:

- Terminal
- Cabinet central processing unit
- Printer
- Disk storage symbol
- CRT screen
- Report printout
- Figure

Each was produced by a writer using the four templates illustrated in Figure 13.2. The dashed lines in the drawings of Figures 13.3 - 13.7 show the parts of the template shapes that were not used. All drawings are full-sized so you can compare them directly to the templates.

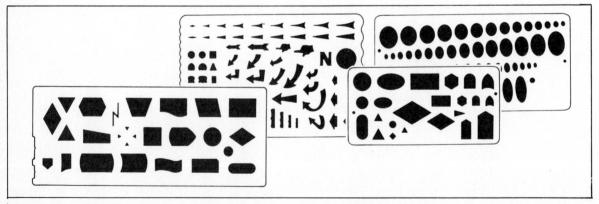

Figure 13.2 Templates used in sample graphics. Those used are the IBM Flowcharting Template (X20-8020), Timely Arrow and Bracket (T-66), Berol RapiDesign Ellipse Master (R-77), and Berol RapiDesign Fault Tree (R-555).

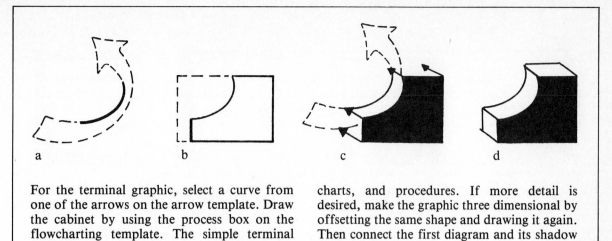

For the terminal graphic, select a curve from one of the arrows on the arrow template. Draw the cabinet by using the process box on the flowcharting template. The simple terminal shape (b) can be used in processing flows, charts, and procedures. If more detail is desired, make the graphic three dimensional by offsetting the same shape and drawing it again. Then connect the first diagram and its shadow with *parallel* lines (c).

Figure 13.3 *Development of a terminal graphic*

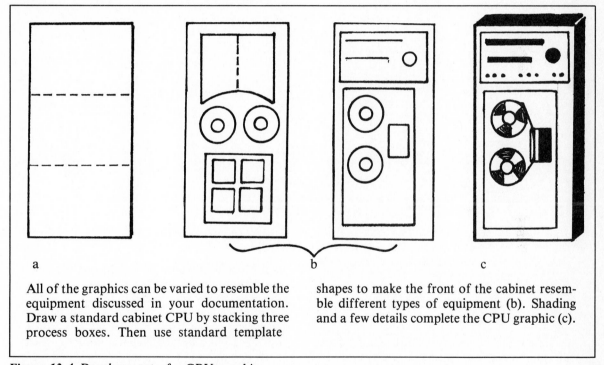

All of the graphics can be varied to resemble the equipment discussed in your documentation. Draw a standard cabinet CPU by stacking three process boxes. Then use standard template shapes to make the front of the cabinet resemble different types of equipment (b). Shading and a few details complete the CPU graphic (c).

Figure 13.4 *Development of a CPU graphic*

Reusing Graphics When developing graphics, always reuse what you have already created. You need not redraw figures or symbols that you have already prepared for another section or another document. A good copy works just as well.

In fact, a good time-saver is to prepare the graphics slightly larger than you need them and make reduction copies of various sizes to paste on your illustrations. The reduction sharpens the lines, and the same graphic can be used to improve the appeal of many sections of your document.

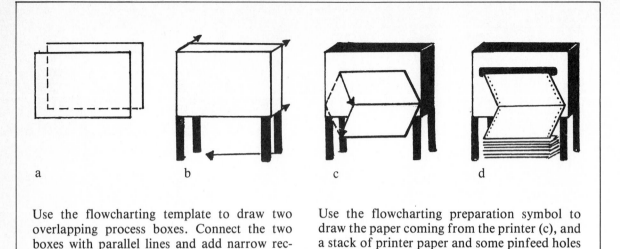

a   b   c   d

Use the flowcharting template to draw two overlapping process boxes. Connect the two boxes with parallel lines and add narrow rectangular legs to complete the printer cabinet.

Use the flowcharting preparation symbol to draw the paper coming from the printer (c), and a stack of printer paper and some pinfeed holes complete the illustration (d).

Figure 13.5 Development of a printer graphic

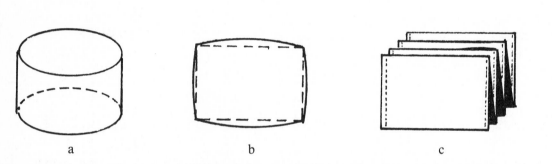

a   b   c

Many diagrams do not need even the simplified equipment graphics illustrated in Figure 13.3 - 13.5. Sometimes all you need is a disk symbol, a CRT screen, or a printout. Create a disk symbol (a) with an ellipse and a straightedge. The disk symbol can be drawn in any size by using the proper ellipse.

To achieve the curved shape of the CRT screen, fill out the appropriate size and shape of rectangle or square with the curves on the ellipse template (b).

To draw a printout symbol (c), use the same overlapping process boxes (or any size rectangle) as the printer cabinet in Figure 13.4. For the printout, use more overlapping rectangles and connect them from the top of one to the bottom of the other to give an accordian effect to the paper.

Figure 13.6 Development of simple representational graphics

Once you have learned the techniques of using the templates to develop graphics, you can combine graphic elements for illustrations and flows throughout the document. The entire flow diagram of Figure 13.8, for example, was created using template shapes and straight lines. The finished diagram was reduced 55% for reproduction.

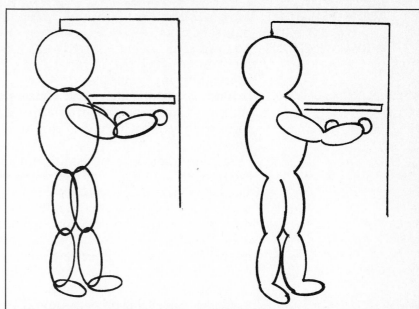

These figures were drawn using the ellipse template and the circle from the fault tree template. With the exception of the torso, which is a 45 degree ellipse, all the ellipses are 25 degrees.

Figure 13.7 Development of figure graphics

Figure 13.8 Combining template graphics

ADDING SHADING TO YOUR ILLUSTRATIONS

Most MIS documents are produced on equipment that can reproduce only solid color — such as black type or black lines on a white page. You can easily include properly sized black and white illustrations, input forms, and output reports in your documentation without causing copying problems.

But what about adding some visual interest to your illustrations — shading to give depth to a drawing or to highlight a special part of a form or the text? This is also easy to do when you use the proper materials.

An illustration or form shaded with a pencil requires special processing or the reproduction equipment either does not pick up the shading or picks it up as black rather than gray. Highlighting must be done with materials that create degrees of shading with patterns of dots or lines. The reproduction equipment sees only the sparse or dense patterns of black dots or lines and, therefore, reproduces the image without special processing. The eye, however, blends the dots or lines into the continuous shades desired.

Hundreds of patterns, textures, and tones to accomplish this shading are available on press-down film. To illustrate the versatility of a single sheet of this material, the four shading samples in Figure 13.9 were produced with a single sheet of 30% fine-line ARTYPE (HR4037). The shades and patterns were created by turning the adhesive sheet as indicated to vary the dot pattern.

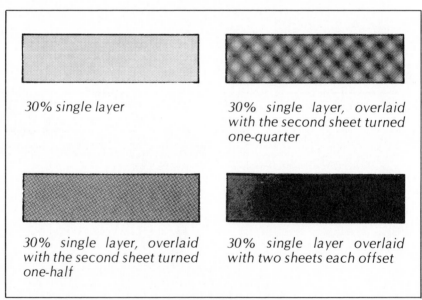

30% single layer

30% single layer, overlaid with the second sheet turned one-quarter

30% single layer, overlaid with the second sheet turned one-half

30% single layer overlaid with two sheets each offset

Figure 13.9 *Varying the dot pattern of shading film*

Application Procedure

Applying the shading material is a simple four-step process that requires little skill and very simple equipment — a razor knife for cutting the material and a burnishing tool for rubbing over the material to make it adhere well.

The four steps are shown in Figure 13.10.

Shading material can be used in user-directed documentation to:
• Add visual interest to illustrations.
• Highlight user input data on a screen or input form.

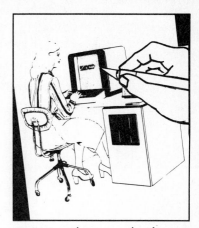

1. Peel away the backing from the adhesive sheet, position it on the area to be shaded, and press it in place.

2. Using the razor knife, cut lightly around the area to be shaded. If you cut through the page, simply tape the cut on the back.

3. Carefully strip away the excess shading material and return it to the backing sheet.

4. Using the burnishing tool, rub over the positioned shading material.

Figure 13.10 Steps in applying shading film

- Subdue surrounding information (for example, on a report) so the data being discussed is easily identified.

STANDARDIZED FORMS

Forms can simplify graphic development. The form in Figure 13.11 was developed for a user's guide with many screen illustrations. The full-sized form provides a screen diagram large enough that screen data can be typed directly on the sheet with a 10-pitch typewriter or the screen can be dumped to a printer and then cut and pasted onto the screen form. The printer must have white paper and a new ribbon. Then reduce the assembled screen to fit the space.

By using a preparation form, you can handle screen figures uniformly in all documents in the project regardless of who prepares the figures.

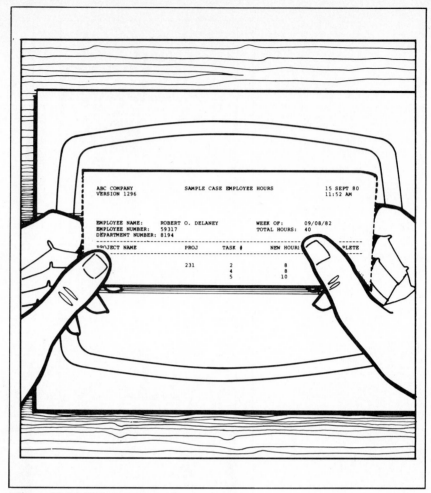

Figure 13.11 Using a screen form

Using Available Illustration Materials

Clip-art and vendor materials are two of the many sources of already prepared graphics and illustrations that can be effectively used in MIS documents. Often, effective designs or graphics can be adapted from advertisements or illustrations in trade magazines. Adaptation, however, is essential because published illustrations and graphics cannot be copied without permission. Photographs are another illustration possibility that should not be overlooked.

This section discusses how to use materials from two sources — clip-out art and photographs.

CLIP-OUT ART

Clip-out books with illustrations for all kinds of situations are available for purchase or loan from a printer or a graphic arts department. These illustrations are generally black-on-white line drawings that you can cut out of the book and paste right on your page.

You need to be flexible when using clip-out art. You may not find exactly what you need. You may have to adapt or combine illustrations or reduce or blow up the graphics, but the clip-out art gives you a good start. Figure 13.12 shows how some clip-out art was adapted to produce a brochure cover design.

Original clip-out art

COMPUTER SUPERVISOR'S OPERATIONS GUIDE

PRESTIGE CORP.

Figure 13.12 Using clip-out art

PHOTOGRAPHS
Photography is often the easiest way to obtain illustrations of equipment and CRT screens. For example, by photographing the screens used by an operator for an online application, the screen information does not have to be typed. Moreover, you ensure that the screens in the manual match exactly what the operator sees.

Photographs, used with great effect in vendor materials, are rare in internal MIS publications. The assumption seems to be that photographs are difficult and expensive to prepare for reproduction.

While it is true that photographs must undergo special preparation before they can be reproduced, a photo copy service can provide this preparation simply and inexpensively. When you receive the prepared copy of your photograph, it is a positive print. You can trim it to size, as needed, and paste it right on the page for reproduction the same as a drawing or typewritten page.

What Instructions
to Give

Preparing photographs for reproduction requires negative/positive photocopying equipment and special paper, such as Kodak PMT (photomechanical transfer) paper. If you ask for a PMT, the photo copy service will know what you want, even though they do not use this particular brand. You must also tell the photo copy service the size you require and whether the photograph is to be screened or unscreened.

Sizing Photographs. The first step in sizing a photograph is determining what parts of it you want to use. You can, for example, decide to show only some of the equipment in a photograph or eliminate unnecessary background. This process is called cropping. Figure 13.13 shows a photograph marked to indicate how it is to be cropped.

The second step is telling the copy service what reduction you want or what the critical dimension is. The critical dimension is either the width or length desired. You should supply only one dimension. This would be the width, for example, if the illustration must fit into a text column. The proportions of the photograph then determine the length.

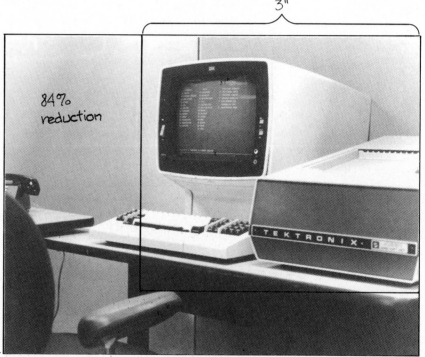

Figure 13.13 Photograph marked for cropping and sizing

Screened Copies. Ask for a screened photo copy when your photographs are of such things as equipment and people and depend on variations of gray tones for their detail.

As shown in Figure 13.14, when a photo is not screened, reproduction equipment cannot capture the gray tones. So during the photo copying process, a screen is placed between the photograph and the copy paper to transform the photo's continuous gray tones into a pattern of dense and sparse dots, which reproduction equipment can handle. The detail of Figure 13.15 shows an enlargement of the dot pattern on a portion of the screened photograph.

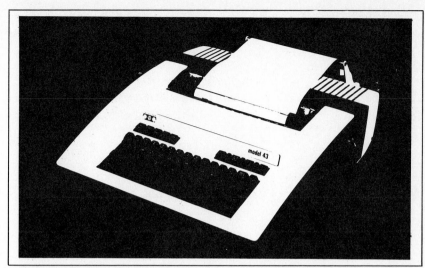

Figure 13.14 Effect of reproducing an unprepared photograph

Figure 13.15 Screened photograph and dot pattern

Unscreened Copies. Photographs that do not require gray tones, such as the CRT display in Figure 13.16, still require preparation to heighten or intensify the contrast between the dark and light areas of the photograph. When the PMT is made without a screen, all the light gray tones, such as the background of the CRT display itself, do not print (drop out), giving a clearer picture of the content. The CRT outline is drawn, not photographed.

Where to Get a Photograph Prepared

Since screened photographic copies are common in internal newsletters and for brochure layouts, most in-house reproduction or graphics departments know where to get screened copies of photographs. If you are seeking a source on your own, look in the Yellow Pages under Photo Copying. Not all shops make screened copies, so call first to check.

Do not let the industry jargon complicate this simple process. Screens, for example, come in various line pattern densities from 65 lines through 133 lines. Your printer or photo copy service can tell

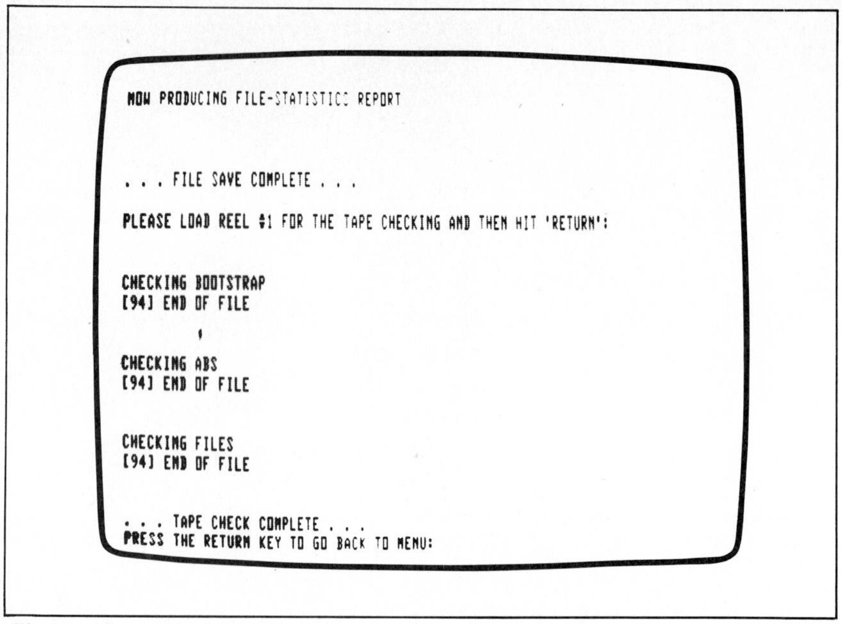

NOW PRODUCING FILE-STATISTICS REPORT

. . . FILE SAVE COMPLETE . . .

PLEASE LOAD REEL #1 FOR THE TAPE CHECKING AND THEN HIT 'RETURN':

CHECKING BOOTSTRAP
[94] END OF FILE

CHECKING ABS
[94] END OF FILE

CHECKING FILES
[94] END OF FILE

. . . TAPE CHECK COMPLETE . . .
PRESS THE RETURN KEY TO GO BACK TO MENU:

Figure 13.16 Unscreened photograph of CRT display

you what line count is best for your paper and printing process. Or you can run several tests on one photograph, getting a sample of all possibilities, and make your own line selection. The charge for preparing black and white photos is nominal. Also, you can group your photographs and print several on the same sheet of photo paper to reduce the cost. For example, one 8″ by 10″ sheet can accommodate four 4″ by 5″ photographs.

What Photographs to Select For internal manuals, an equipment vendor is usually willing to provide the equipment photographs you require. A competent photographer can take any other necessary photographs in a day or less of shooting if you have compiled a list of the photos you need from your figure control list.

Select or specify black and white photographs the same size as or larger than you need in the document. When the photographic copy is made, the photograph can be reduced to the specified size.

Reducing the photograph clarifies the detail. The CRT screen in Figure 13.16 was photographed with a 4″ by 5″ view camera with a polaroid back and high-speed film (ASA 400). To overcome the curvature of the screen, the photographer mounted the camera on a tripod with the back of the camera parallel to the screen. During photo copying, the original was reduced to 90% to clarify the print detail.

Working with a Graphic Artist

When graphic and illustration needs are complicated or time is short, the best solution may be a graphic artist. To save time and money, the graphic artist can prepare rough sketches for all review copies. Following the review of the figure content, he prepares the finished art. Using a graphic artist does not mean you must go outside your company. Your company may have graphic support in one of the

following departments:
- Graphic arts
- Publications
- Advertising or marketing

- Engineering
- Reproduction
- Marketing

DEVELOPING SOURCE MATERIAL

Good preparation of materials for a graphic artist is a must. You understand your material much better than the artist does. As a result, you can more easily select the important points to illustrate and can summarize what to include in the illustrations.

Good preparation saves you time on corrections. With clear instructions before he begins, the artist is less likely to make a mistake requiring additional hours of correction time.

Good source material for a graphic artist does not mean that you must lay out the brochure or draw the figure for him. It means that you must provide samples, sketches, or written explanations that clearly indicate what it is you want for your finished document.

If, for example, you are planning a marketing brochure, show your artist samples of other brochures and point out what you like and do not like about each. For illustrations, provide a sketch or a clearly written explanation of what you want.

In Figure 13.17, (A) shows the writer's sketch, (B) is the artist's first rough, (C) shows the writer's corrections to the rough, and (D) is the final illustration.

Figure 13.17 Development of an illustration by a graphic artist

Note that the writer's rough sketch covered both content of the illustration and size requirements for the finished art. However, the explanation was not clear whether the accountant in the figure should be male or female. The artist had no way of knowing.

If you are having trouble finding good source material for your artist and are not sure that he understands what you are asking for, ask him to prepare a limited sample. Ask for a page spread in the format, one illustration, or a detailed layout to help you determine, with limited expense, whether you are communicating your intentions for the finished document.

REVIEWING FINISHED ART

Reviewing the work of a graphic artist is the same as reviewing any other work. First, check it for accuracy and completeness; then, for quality. You should not accept anything that does not meet your standards. If type is too small or columns too uneven or if illustrations are in the wrong style, ask the artist to make corrections. You sought graphic support originally to ensure that the piece would look impressive. Do not accept anything less than your goal.

In Conclusion

Figures and illustrations in MIS documents can vary from simple representations of reports to complicated diagrams. The level of complexity depends on the needs of the document and the availability of illustration material and graphic support.

The amount of preparation required depends on the source of the illustration. If, for example, a graphic artist prepares the figure and he has been briefed properly, the finished figure should be ready for positioning in the document with no additional preparation. Figures from other sources always need some special preparation, even though it may involve only reduction of a figure to the proper size.

Part 6
Production

Without production, a document exists only as a writer's personal copy. Production prepares the document for distribution.

Production occurs throughout development. It involves page preparation, reproduction, and assembly of the material. Production may mean preparing interim copies for review and field testing or publishing the final document.

Every DDM task calls for some degree of production skill. Production coordination skills are particularly important whenever you turn materials over to a support service. Three tasks directly involve production coordination.

- Task 1 - Plan Documentation Project
- Task 2 - Plan Document Content
- Task 10 - Coordinate Publication

During planning, you plan production and production control. When the final draft is approved, you coordinate the publication of the document.

Chapters 14, 15, and 16 discuss the production coordination activities needed to complete these tasks.

Chapter 14 - Production Control
The writer is typically the production controller, making sure that support services know what to do and that the work gets done on time and correctly. This chapter presents guidelines for production control and working with support services.

Chapter 15 - Production Methods
In making requests of support services, you should know something about their methods. This chapter explains two approaches to preparing pages for reproduction and summarizes two commonly used reproduction methods. Then it suggests a way to supervise the assembly of the material.

Chapter 16 - Project Wrap-Up
When the document is printed and assembled, the natural reaction for a writer is to assume the project is completed. To complete the development project properly, however, you must coordinate document distribution and prepare for the eventual updating of the document. This chapter discusses these project wrap-up topics.

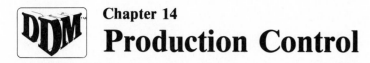

Chapter 14
Production Control

Chapter 14
Production Control

During project planning, you determine production requirements. As work on a document progresses, you:
- Keep track of where each element of the document is at any given time.
- Work with support services to type the material, prepare figures, order supplies, and reproduce copies.

Tracking Development

Typically, document development occurs on several levels at once. Some sections are in word processing; some are being written; others are in preliminary review or revision. Illustrations and figures may be in the print shop for reduction, with the graphics department for artwork, or in the computer center's printout queue. Thus, controlling production is essential for publishing materials on schedule.

Control forms can help track each document, document part, and figure throughout development. Additionally, these forms serve as a reference for monitoring schedule commitments and reporting progress. They are a source of production information for improving time estimates for future projects.

You design control forms during document planning after the support services requirements and the development schedule are known. At minimum, you need a development control form to track material throughout development and a figure control list to track the development of figures. You may also need a word processing log.

DEVELOPMENT CONTROL FORM

Lay out your form to include all the checkpoints in the development scenario. Figure 14.1 shows a sample development control form based on the development schedule presented in Figure 5.5. This form assumes that the completion date of one step is the start date of the next step. If the materials spend time in transit, it might be necessary to include both start and end dates.

FIGURE CONTROL LIST

Figure 14.1 tracks each section of the document through the development. Specific graphics within these sections also require production control as they go from graphic idea or rough sketches through graphic arts, typing, and so forth. The sample figure control list shown in Figure 14.2 tracks graphic development after you have identified the figures.

① Accounting System User's Guide   DEVELOPMENT CONTROL FORM   **Lee Arnold**
(publication)   (writer)

Chris Pauly   **2241**
(word processing)   (ext)

DATES ARE COMPLETE DATES.
The complete date of one task
is the IN date to the next
task.

② ③	WRITE FIRST DRAFT; DEVELOP GRAPHICS	TYPE FIRST DRAFT	TECHNICAL REVIEW	REWRITE DRAFT; COMPLETE GRAPHICS	TYPE THE REWRITE CORRECTIONS	USER REVIEW	INCORPORATE USER COMMENTS	TYPE THE CORRECTIONS; PRE-PARE FINAL DRAFT	REVIEW FINAL DRAFT	MAKE FINAL CORRECTIONS	PRINT THE COPIES	ASSEMBLE THE COPIES
Development Schedule	2/19	3/5	3/12	4/9	4/16	4/30	5/7	5/12	5/14	5/18	6/1	6/3 ④
Preface												
1. Introduction	2/22 ⑥											
2. Pre-input Planning	2/19											
3. Input	1/13	1/21										
4. Processing	2/15	2/22										
5. Output	1/26	1/29										
6. Sample Problem	2/24											
7. Batch Procedures	1/18	1/25										

⑤ ⑦

① General information at the top of the form lists the publication title, writer, and contact person for word processing.
② Development checkpoints are listed across the page to form columns.
③ Target dates are listed for the development checkpoints.

④ The last date is the targeted completion date for the project.
⑤ Chapters or sections to be completed are listed down the side.
⑥ The actual completion date is entered above the dashed line.
⑦ A graphic representation of progress can be kept by filling in the area below the dashed line.

Figure 14.1 Development control form

As you identify graphics during Task 5, Write First Draft, start filling in the figure control list and add to it during Task 6, Develop Graphics and Task 8, Rewrite and Complete Graphics.

You can also track the ordering of binders, tabs, and paper on the figure control list.

WORD PROCESSING LOG

If you are responsible for proofreading, you may send material to word processing several times during a single development activity. A word processing log can help you track material in and out of word processing. A sample log form is shown in Figure 14.3.

Each time you give material to word processing, record the IN date. When you receive the typed material, record the OUT date.

™ of Sandra Pakin & Associates, Inc.

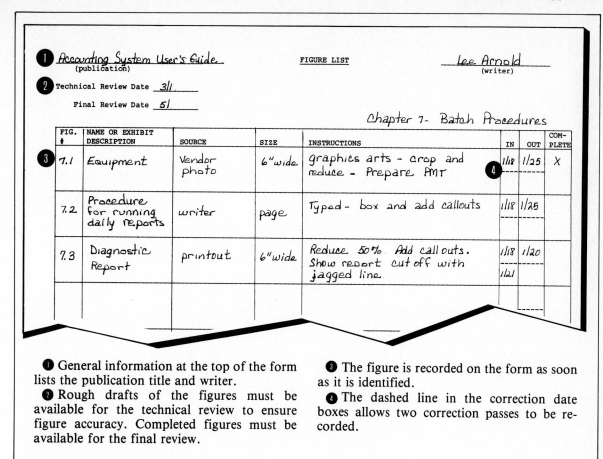

1 *Accounting System User's Guide*
(publication)

FIGURE LIST

Lee Arnold
(writer)

2 Technical Review Date _3/1_

Final Review Date _5/_

Chapter 7- Batch Procedures

FIG. #	NAME OR EXHIBIT DESCRIPTION	SOURCE	SIZE	INSTRUCTIONS	IN	OUT	COM- PLETE
3 7.1	Equipment	Vendor photo	6" wide	graphics arts - crop and reduce - Prepare AMT **4**	1/18	1/25	X
7.2	Procedure for running daily reports	writer	page	Typed - box and add callouts	1/18	1/25	
7.3	Diagnostic Report	printout	6" wide	Reduce 50%. Add call outs. Show report cut off with jagged line.	1/18 1/21	1/20	

1 General information at the top of the form lists the publication title and writer.

2 Rough drafts of the figures must be available for the technical review to ensure figure accuracy. Completed figures must be available for the final review.

3 The figure is recorded on the form as soon as it is identified.

4 The dashed line in the correction date boxes allows two correction passes to be recorded.

Figure 14.2 Figure control list

WORD PROCESSING LOG   PAGE _1_

SECTION NUMBER AND TITLE	DOC #	INITIAL TYPING	REVISION #1	REVISION #2	REVISION #3	REVISION #4	REVISION #5	DONE
1. Introduction	1733F	IN 2/22 OUT	IN OUT	IN OUT	IN OUT	IN OUT	IN OUT	
2. Pre-Input Planning	1692F	IN 2/19 OUT 2/22	IN 2/24 OUT	IN OUT	IN OUT	IN	IN	

Figure 14.3 Word processing log

Working with Support Services

During project planning, you:
- Identify the production support resources needed at each development checkpoint.
- Find out how work is scheduled and submitted.

- Decide with the support service how you will notify each other if a due date cannot be met.

You use all of this information as you work with the support services to produce your document. You must:

- Prepare the material for submission.
- Schedule the service and submit the work with the proper work request form.
- Provide instructions on your requirements.
- Check the completed work.

PREPARING MATERIAL
FOR SUBMISSION

Each support service may have specific requirements about the preparation of material for submission. If they do not, follow the suggestions in this section.

For Word Processing

To help the typists do a better job with your material:

- Mark the first few pages of a new document with complete format notes, especially indenting and line spacing.
- Mark any unusual spacing requirements, including the number of line spaces to leave for figures. (There are six lines to the inch.)
- Mark any special typing that you need — for example, whether a word is supposed to be all caps. This is especially important if you are submitting handwritten material.
- Use the correction marks preferred by your typist. For example, some typists prefer to have deleted material circled. Others prefer a line drawn through the words to be omitted.

For Graphic Arts

To help graphic arts do a better job with your material:

- Provide a sample of what you are trying to achieve, whenever possible.
- List size and style requirements for each figure.
- Ask for rough sketches first.

For Reproduction
Services

To help reproduction services do a better job of copying your material:

- Be sure all pages are in their correct order.
- For two-sided printing, mark the back of each page with a page number and indicate whether the page is a front page or a back page. For example, if A indicates a front page and B indicates a back page, the first four sheets are numbered 1A, 1B, 2A, 2B. If the back of a page should be blank, either leave off the letter designator or insert a blank sheet for the B page.
- If you want a colored sheet inserted at the beginning of each chapter, write a note on a colored sheet and place it within the material.

For Purchasing

Purchasing should be able to supply you with catalogs and samples of the various supplies you want ordered. They need to know what kind of supplies you need and special requirements. For example:

- Binders
  - Size of binder — from 1/2 inch to 3 inches
  - Ring style — D-ring or round ring
  - Paper lifters
  - Inside pockets
  - Cover treatment — plain, silk-screened, clear plastic cover into which you insert a printed cover sheet
  - Color

- Tabs
  - Number of tabs in a set
  - Printing for each tab
  - Color
- Paper
  - Color and weight
  - Preprinting

SCHEDULING AND
SUBMITTING WORK

Follow the support services scheduling procedures. If after you have scheduled some work, you are unable to deliver it on time, be sure to notify the support service so they can adjust their work accordingly.

When you are ready to submit the work, use the required work submittal form. Be sure to add as a special instruction that you want to be notified if the material will not be ready by the due date.

If the service has no submittal form, write a memo. Figure 14.4

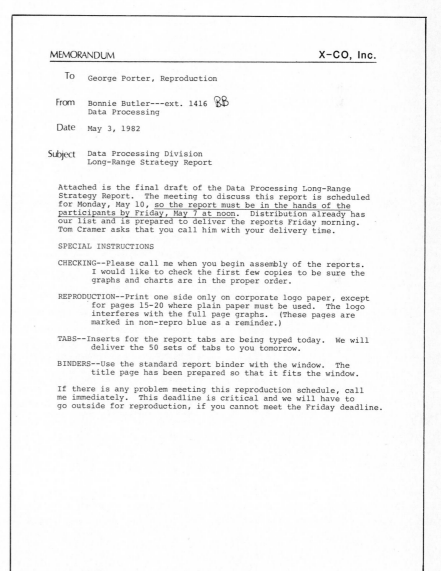

Figure 14.4 Submitting work with a memo

shows a sample transmittal memo, which contains:

- Name of the project.
- Type of work requested.
- For reproduction services and purchasing, number of copies or supplies needed.
- Due date. Never use ASAP (as soon as possible) as a due date. Its meaning is unclear. It could mean "as quickly as possible" or "anytime you get to it."
- Request to be notified if the due date cannot be met.
- Contact name and extension.
- Specific instructions for performing the work.

PROVIDING INSTRUCTIONS

The first time you use a support service for a document, you need to brief the person or persons doing the work. Always prepare written instructions and review those instructions with the support service.

Briefing the Typist

Prepare typing instructions based on your page format. The typing

---

```
TYPING INSTRUCTIONS FOR ALL VERSIONS OF
THE MULTI-TIME SYSTEM DOCUMENTATION

These instructions include the following information:

1-2    Text typing instructions
3      Text typing format sheet
4      Figure typing instructions and sample figure
5-7    Sample typed pages
8      Text correction symbols

TEXT TYPING INSTRUCTIONS

In addition to the text and figures, the elements that appear on every
page include:

    o    Chapter title in the upper right-hand corner
    o    Publication code and date in the lower left-hand corner
    o    Page number in the lower right-hand corner

All pages are to follow the standard margins and text positioning
indicated on the text typing format sheet on page 3.

Headlines are typed in a hierarchy format as follows:

    CHAPTER HEADLINES are all caps, centered on the page, and
        underlined.  Chapters always begin down six carriage returns
        from the normal top text margin as indicated by the dotted
        line on the text format sheet.

    SECTION HEADLINES are all caps with no underline.

    Topic Headlines are caps and lower case and underlined.

Section and topic headlines are typed in the left-hand margin only
which may require the headlines to be typed on more than one line.  The
headline begins even with the beginning of the paragraph and should be
divided so they make sense.  Words cannot be divided in headlines.  For
examples of how headlines should be typed on multiple lines, see the
page samples on pages 5-7.

Text and headlines are to be typed using the Courier style on the
10-pitch typewriter.  Elements within the text that are underlined
should be typed in italics, using the Courier italic.

The first paragraph of a section is not to be indented.  All remaining
paragraphs in the section are to be indented three spaces.  Additional
indenting is required as follows:

    o    Bullet and number lists--indent three spaces to the bullet or
         number and four spaces after

    o    Sub-items in a bullet or number list--indent four spaces and
         type a hyphen, then indent three more spaces for the text

    o    Highlighted and summary paragraphs--indent three spaces from
         each side

                              -- 1 --
```

Figure 14.5 Typing instructions

instructions explain for the typist:

- Placement of elements on the page — such as margins, headers and footers, tabs.
- Typing style for standard text items — such as headings, text, figures, tables of contents, examples within the text.
- Size and style of type to use and when to use specialized type, such as italics or bold face, if these are available.
- Symbols you use to mark corrections.

You might also give the typist a copy of the project writing guide. Figure 14.5 shows sample typing instructions.

Briefing the Graphic Artist

The section, "Working with a Graphic Artist," in Chapter 13 describes this support service. In addition, when you bring materials to the graphic artist for the first time, go over:

- Purpose of the document
- Graphic approach

Briefing Reproduction Services

With reproduction services, review:

- Type of paper
- Ink color
- Number of copies
- Printing — one-sided or two-sided
- Collating needs, such as colored paper between chapters

CHECKING THE RETURNED MATERIAL

You are responsible for checking all materials returned to you. You need to check that:

- All the material is complete and in the proper order.
- Work is accurate and readable.
- All requested formatting and corrections are complete.

Additionally, if the word processing unit does not provide proofreading, you must proofread the material. If they do proofread, you may want to spot-check their proofreading, and you should check the final word processing before you submit the draft for reproduction.

Proofreading

Proofreading is matching *word for word* the original copy against the typed copy. The most accurate proofreading takes place when two people proofread, one to read the draft aloud and the second to check the finished text. No editing changes are made during proofreading, but many critical errors can be corrected. For example, consider the importance of catching the following typing errors:

- A proposed cost of $105,000 in a marketing brochure is mistyped as $15,000.
- A list of required JCL omits a card or even a comma delimiter.
- Two steps in a recommended procedure in an operator's guide are transposed.

For technical material, such as coding examples, you may also have to use a ruler to measure spacing.

Checklist for Production Control

Preparation for production control begins when you determine the project's production requirements during project planning. In document planning, you develop a development control form based on the development schedule, and you begin tracking the development of the document after approval of the document plan.

The following checklist identifies production control activities.

DURING DOCUMENT PLANNING
☐ Design development control form.
☐ Design figure control list.
☐ Design word processing log, if needed.

DURING ALL OTHER DEVELOPMENT ACTIVITIES
☐ Use the forms to track production.
☐ Schedule work as needed.
☐ Prepare the material for submission.
☐ Fill out the proper work submittal form or write a memo.
☐ Brief the support service on your requirements and supply written instructions.
☐ Check the returned work.

Chapter 15
Production Methods

of Sandra Pakin & Associates, Inc.

Chapter 15
Production Methods

Production consists of page preparation, reproduction, and assembly of the copied material. This chapter discusses two ways to prepare pages for reproduction and two ways to reproduce the material. It also explains your responsibilities associated with each. Finally, this chapter discusses how to coordinate assembly of the material if a reproduction service does not do it.

Page Preparation

Two methods for preparing pages for production are:
- Mark up and insert
- Cut apart and paste up

MARK UP AND INSERT The mark-up-and-insert method is the preparation method most often used for typed documents. Before producing any pages, you determine the size and arrangement of the inserts to go into the text. You instruct the typist to leave space for them in the appropriate places in the typescript. You, a secretary in your department, the word processing unit, or a graphic artist then pastes down the illustrations.

CUT APART AND PASTE UP The cut-apart-and-paste-up method of page preparation is usually used when typesetting is substituted for word processing or pages are to be designed with special text placement. Normally, you do not typeset the material until it is through user review or field testing. Until then, you type the pages and prepare them using the mark-up-and-insert method.

The basic procedure for cut apart and paste up is:
- All the text is typeset in continuous columns of the proper width for the finished page.
- All headings and text elements that cannot be set with the text are produced separately.
- Illustrations are prepared and photostated to the proper size.
- All the elements are cut apart, arranged, and pasted up on illustration boards. This process is also called keylining or make-ready. Figure 15.1 shows the way the elements for a fanfold reference summary card are arranged. The back and front pages are on side 1 of the unfolded card. Notice that the front page of the reference card is the rightmost column. The entire inside of the card is on side 2.

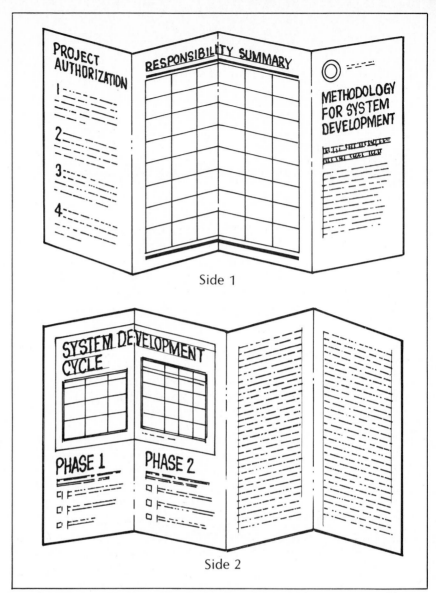

Figure 15.1 Layout for an eight-page reference summary card. An illustration board is prepared for each side.

A graphic artist generally prepares the pages on illustration boards. Your responsibilities are to properly submit and check the work. Checking takes two passes:

- Read the galleys (pages of type) to correct typographical and content errors.
- Review the boards to correct paste-up errors.

Checking the galleys is the same as proofreading any text. Make sure that all the words are in the proper order. You may also make content changes, but you should hold these to a minimum. Figure 15.2 shows a corrected galley from this book.

When the boards are returned to you for corrections, mark on either:

- Tissue that the artist places over the boards.
- Copy of the boards.

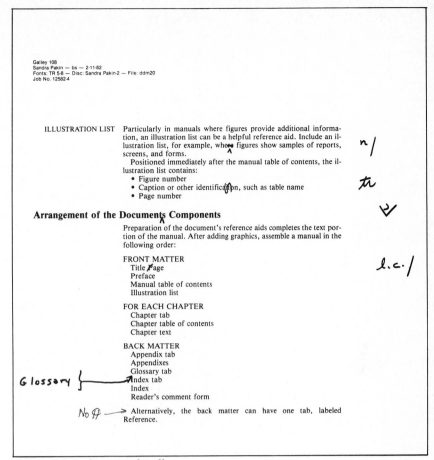

Figure 15.2 Corrected galley

Never mark on the finished page, or the artist will have to redo the page instead of making a correction. Change only what you must. Content changes at this time are time-consuming and expensive.

For a complicated document, such as a center-stapled brochure, the graphic artist should prepare a prototype. For a prototype, the artist puts together copies of the layout pages to look like the finished document.

The prototype allows you to make a last check on the material to ensure that:

- Text logically follows from one page to the next.
- Page spreads are coordinated and discussions of figures are on the same or facing pages.
- Page numbers, headers, and footers are correct and headings are accurately reflected in the table of contents.

Reproduction Methods

To help you understand what you need to know about the reproduction method to be used on your material, this section discusses two common methods:

- Copy machine reproduction
- Offset printing

COPY MACHINE
REPRODUCTION

Documents can be reproduced on an office copy machine or submitted to an in-house department or a firm that specializes in copying. You need to know the capabilities of the copy machine *before* you prepare the pages. Ask about or test for the following:

- How illustrations reproduce.
- How the machine reproduces items pasted or taped on the page.
- Whether the copy machine works with letterhead paper.
- Whether the copier can do two-sided copying.

Reproduction of Illustrations. To determine how well your illustrations reproduce, test a sample of each illustration type. Some machines, for example, cannot reproduce computer printout paper because the shaded lines come out too dark to read the data printed on them. In this case, you have to type the reports or have them printed on plain paper. You should also check what type of shading material, if any, works with the copier.

Reproduction of Pasted Items. Check how the machine reproduces items pasted on the page, because some machines show a distinct black line where the edge of the pasted-down paper is. In this case, either you have to cut the illustration so the figure outline coincides with the edge of the pasted-down figure, or you have to go over the paper edge with white tape or correction fluid.

Reproduction of Letterhead. At times you may want to produce a report or document on a letterhead or form paper. Most plain paper copiers that use standard-sized paper can accommodate letterhead paper. Machines that use roll or special process paper cannot take a letterhead. For these, prepare each page on letterhead paper. However, before preparing all the pages on the letterhead, test it on the copier to be sure it yields a good clean image. A gold logo, for example, may copy with a muddy gray look.

Two-sided Copying. If you are producing a lengthy document, such as a manual or major report, two-sided reproduction cuts down the volume of paper and makes your document appear more compact. Before you decide on two-sided copying, be sure that your:

- Copier can copy on both sides. Roll-type copiers and some plain paper copiers cannot do two-sided reproduction.
- Copier can take a quality of paper that does not have show-through, where images from the other side are visible under normal reading conditions.

OFFSET PRINTING

Offset printing uses a plate made from a photograph of a page to print the required number of copies. With offset printing, you can use any kind of black-on-white text or illustrations and a wide range of shading materials.

During project planning when you prepare your production requirements, you can ask reproduction services about the kind of shading material to use, any special requirements for illustrations, and procedures for making corrections. You should also find out:

- Type of available paper.
- Type of proofs you receive.

Type of Paper

A wide range of types, colors, and weights of paper is available with offset printing. The paper should meet the needs of the document. For example, a reference card is best printed on heavier paper. The

188

color of the card can coordinate with the binder color. For example, if the binders are dark blue, you might select a light blue color for the cards.

For manuals, paper selection is also important. For example, when manuals are to be used in a plant or factory location or have a long projected life, grease resistant paper should be considered. You can also consider texture and quality of the paper, the shade if you do not want pure white, and its ability to take two-sided reproduction. Reproduction services or purchasing can help you make the appropriate paper selection.

Proofs With offset printing and many other reproduction methods, the printer can run a proof of the document once he has prepared the printing plates and *before* he prints the document. Whenever you have a document requiring an additional color, be sure to request a color key proof. A color key proof lets you determine that the printer has properly placed the color.

When you review the proof, you should look first for printer errors. For example, check that:

- Assembly is correct. The printer's proof should be in the same order and look the same as the pages of the final document. You can quickly check whether the printer understands how to assemble the pages and has the plates set up correctly so that pages line up across top and bottom margins.
- Reproduction is acceptable. Good reproduction means that all the detail on the figures shows up and all the letters are clear without broken or incomplete letters. Also check that the density of print is even over all the pages without some areas being significantly lighter or darker than others.

Additionally, the proof is a valuable last-chance check on accuracy that you should take if it is available. Corrections at this stage of production, however, are very costly because it means redoing the plates. Any corrections must be carefully considered and style corrections should not be allowed.

Assembly of the Material

After reproduction comes assembling of the copies. The reproduction service may handle assembly, especially when it involves some form of permanent binding or stapling. In this case, the prototype and printer's proofs serve as preliminary checks on assembly. For complicated documents, you may want to be present when assembly begins so you can recheck the first assembled copies.

When the reproduction service does not assemble the final material, you are responsible for the assembly. You do not have to do the actual assembling. Personal involvement in the actual assembly should occur only for smaller projects or projects with a critical time problem, because it is not an effective use of your time.

Instead, use clerical or temporary help to do the work. Provide for them:

- Complete instructions for assembling the material and checking all assembled documents.
- All materials — the reproduced copies, binders, folders, staplers, tabs, and so forth.
- Prototype, completely assembled.

In Conclusion

A support service usually performs page preparation and reproduction. Your responsibilities include providing complete and accurate instructions and checking the completed work. You are also responsible for the quality of the original. The reproduced copy can be only as good as the original you submitted. Text typed with a poor ribbon or smudged or messy illustrations can compromise the quality of the printed material.

Chapter 16
Project Wrap-Up

Chapter 16
Project Wrap-Up

Following the reproduction and assembly of the document, you must ensure proper distribution. Additionally, for manuals and some reports, you must prepare for the eventual updating of the material.

Preparation for Distribution

During document planning, you defined distribution requirements. The requirements include determining the distribution method — for example, drop-shipping documents to local offices for distribution by the local system coordinator or sending a copy via inter-office mail to each person on the distribution list. You also decided how much control to maintain over each document. For example, you may elect to mark each copy with a control number and/or have each recipient of the material send back an acknowledgment that he received it.

While you are having the material reproduced and assembled, you should prepare your distribution list and write the distribution memo.

PREPARING THE DISTRIBUTION LIST

A distribution list is simply a list of who should receive or has received a document. The distribution list for drop-shipped material contains the ship-to person's name, title, address, and telephone number and the number of copies he receives. As an added control, you might add the distribution date.

For material delivered to each person individually, the distribution list might contain the following information:
- Person's name, title, address, and telephone number.
- Control number on the document given to that person.
- Space for the date the acknowledgment was returned.

A master correction copy of the distribution list should be kept with the document inventory. This correction copy can be annotated whenever additional copies of the document are taken out of inventory. Remove from the distribution list the names of people who have returned their documents or who are no longer with the company. As you find out about name, address, or telephone number changes, annotate the master correction copy. Before each new distribution, use the master correction copy to update the distribution list.

WRITING THE
DISTRIBUTION MEMO

Some form of transmittal letter or memo should accompany the distribution. For drop-shipped materials, the memo should include:
- Contents of the shipment
- Handling instructions
- Contact name, address, and phone number

For materials distributed to individuals, the memo should include:
- Name and purpose of the document.
- Instructions regarding the material. For example, you must explain how to return the receipt acknowledgment or if the material is an update to an existing manual, how to insert the update and what to do with the replaced pages.
- Contact name, address, and telephone number.

Preparation for Update

Preparation for update begins in project planning when you determine what control information to include in the page format. When you prepare and maintain the project writing guide, you are ensuring that the writer responsible for updating will be able to update the document properly.

With distribution of the document, you can finish preparing for updating:
- Build history and update files from the project file.
- Provide additional updating information.
- Set up a master correction copy of the document.

HISTORY AND
UPDATE FILES

To prepare for updates, you must divide the project file into a history file and an update file. The history file contains background information, and the update file stores all materials useful for updating.

History File

In case of questions about document content, store the following items in a history file:
- First draft of the document as a record of your first approach to the writing project.
- All correspondence, review comments, and marked pages that chart significant changes to the document during the writing development. Give the name of the reviewer with his comments.
- Any critical source material that would be hard to replace or that represents contested points.

Label this material clearly so its purpose can be understood later. This material is history and may never be needed. Box and store it outside of the normal office. Mark it with a review date and a date after which it can be destroyed. For user documentation, the destruction date generally coincides with the life of the current system.

Update File

The update file provides information any writer would need when making changes and rewriting the document. Include the following items from the project file:
- List of all technical and administrative personnel who worked on the project and their contributions and responsibilities.
- Document plan, which contains the purpose, scope, and audiences for the document so that all changes fit into the intent of the document.
- Project writing guide, including specifications for all artwork

and type, so additions or corrections can be compatible with current material.
- Reproduction copy of all pages and illustrations.
- Storage location of any word processing media related to the publication and the storage location of the history file, in case of update questions.

ADDITIONAL
INFORMATION

Additionally, the update file should include a cross-reference list and writer's notes. Also, if you receive reader's comment forms, put a copy of each along with your response in the update file.

Cross-Reference List

A cross-reference list is an index to the cross-references within a document. When you update, you use this list to locate all pages or sections that refer to material you are changing.

An easy way to maintain a cross-reference list is to prepare 3″ by 5″ index cards for each section in the document. The cards, as shown in Figure 16.1, list all references to the section in the manual and all other sections referred to from this one.

SECTION 2.5 PAYROLL DAILY REPORTS

| referred to in: | | refers to: | |

SECTION 2.6 PAYROLL MONTH-END REPORT

referred to in:		refers to:	
Section 1.5	page 10	Section 2.4	page 28
3.4	44	2.7	32
4.6	57	2.8	35
4.7	59		
4.8	61		
7.1	94		

Figure 16.1 Cross-reference cards

Writer's Notes

You may not be the updating writer, or you may not remember development details when it comes time to update the document. Therefore, it is important to note any special development information the updater may need. For example, if illustrations use a master list of names, the updater should know the names and their use.

MASTER
CORRECTION COPY

Not every error in a document requires update. A typographical error, for instance, may be annoying to the reader, but usually does not affect his understanding of the material. However, you should record every error and correct it when you update the material. The best way to record corrections is on a master copy of the document.

Label one copy of the document the master correction copy and note all corrections and update information on this copy as you learn about them. It also helps to put a paper clip on each page that has notes on it so you can quickly review required changes.

In Conclusion

When you develop a manual, always keep in mind that it will probably require updating to correct information or to keep it current with system changes. When a section of the manual changes, you should check the following items:

- Table of contents. Check the table of contents to verify that page numbers for the updated sections are still valid. If not, update the table of contents. Similarly, correct the illustration list if the update includes illustrations.
- Index. If available, use a copy of the index sorted by page numbers to locate quickly items affected by page changes. Make these changes on the alphabetic index listing and add items for any pages added to the document.
- Glossary. Add new terms to the glossary as a result of additions to the manual and review the glossary to delete terms that are no longer applicable.
- Cross-references. Check all cross-references to be sure that sections being referred to have not been deleted or changed.

Appendix A
Sample Project Plan

The project plan for this book begins on the next page. Since the documentation project consists of a single document, the requirements statement portion of the document plan was incorporated into the project plan.

The project plan is not part of the document and is not reviewed for style or adherence to format standards. Instead, it is a statement of the planned direction for the document's development. But the finished project plan does include material — like the topic overview — that can serve as a basis for the document's preface.

© of Sandra Pakin & Associates, Inc.

DDM: The Documentation Development Methodology
PROJECT PLAN
Requirements Statement

TOPIC OVERVIEW

The Documentation Development Methodology (DDM) is a structured approach for developing all types of formal written materials. It consists of ten tasks that divide the documentation development process into containable units of work beginning with planning and following through with review, writing, graphic development, and production. Each DDM task has a defined product and builds on the output of the previous task.

The DDM is a proven means of producing effective documentation. It is a methodology for people committed to producing good documentation. It is not for writers looking for a quick-and-dirty way to produce documentation.

PURPOSE AND SCOPE OF THE BOOK

DDM: The Documentation Development Methodology is being developed to explain the DDM to MIS (management information systems) professionals and to provide them with the background necessary to perform the DDM tasks. To demonstrate the practicality of the DDM, the book will use examples and illustrations from all types of MIS documents. However, the major emphasis of the book is on producing manuals, since smaller-sized documents require a subset of the development activities to be discussed.

This book is not intended to turn a programmer, analyst, or MIS manager into a professional writer. Instead, it is designed to demonstrate how clear, understandable materials can be produced by all levels of MIS professionals.

AUDIENCES
Primary Audience:

MIS professionals are the main audience for the book, whether they work for a company that has a computer or for a hardware or software vendor. In most companies, the MIS professional is responsible for developing all documentation associated with an application or system.

The MIS professional is typically disinterested in documentation and sees it as one of the less appealing aspects of systems development. He rarely has any training in writing. On the positive side, the MIS professional can usually organize things well and looks for efficient ways to do his work.

In presenting this book to the MIS professional, we should assume that he is doing significant work that requires documenting. Examples should reflect realistic system situations.

When he has finished this book, the MIS professional should be able to develop documentation that is recognizably better than anything he has previously produced. He should have increased confidence in his ability to develop good documentation and a basis for continuing improvement of his documentation skills.

Secondary Audience:

Students attending MIS writing courses, end-users who are responsible for producing their own documentation, and MIS technical writers make up the secondary audience of the book.

Students may have difficulty with the book because they do not understand the work environment of the MIS professional. End-users and MIS technical writers may need a greater emphasis on information-gathering techniques than the book provides.

On the other hand, the book provides information on documentation development that is available from no other source.

Tertiary Audience:

College students in technical writing courses are the third audience for the book. While the DDM is applicable to any technical writing, the book assumes a reader familiar with MIS organization and issues, and its examples are specifically and exclusively MIS examples. Teachers may be reluctant to assign the book for this reason and for one other. The DDM and the book de-emphasize writing skill as the key ingredient to producing good documentation. In the DDM, planning and reviewing are of equal importance with writing. Additionally, the DDM recommends graphic approaches to the presentation of material rather than straight text.

Development Requirements

DEVELOPMENT SCENARIO

After the project plan is approved:

Development

1. Prepare extended outline.
2. Review the plan and revise it.
3. Write the first draft and develop graphics.
4. Review the first draft for technical accuracy.
5. Rewrite the draft.
6. Review the rewrite.
7. Rewrite and complete the graphic content.
8. Edit.

Production

9. Prepare page layouts and determine type specifications for the typeset version.
10. Get quotes on typesetting and paste-up and make a vendor selection.
11. Have graphic artist prepare cover design and illustrations not done in-house.
12. Make final corrections and spec the text for typesetting.
13. Get quotes from printers.
14. Submit for typesetting.
15. Order binders, tabs, and mailing cartons.
16. Proofread galleys.
17. Size pages, including space for figures.
18. Submit for paste-up.
19. Check prototype.
20. Prepare the index and submit for typesetting.
21. Check the index.
22. Submit for printing.
23. Check proof.

REVIEW REQUIREMENTS

Reviewers:

Plan - SP&A principals
First draft - SP&A principals, SP&A staff
Rewrite - SP&A principals, user
Edit - SP&A editor

Review Meetings:

Copies will be distributed at a staff meeting and review requirements will be discussed. A special meeting will be held with all reviewers, including the user, to discuss comments. Marked-up copies of the book will be turned in to the rewriter. Two weeks will be allowed for each review.

Production Requirements

WORD PROCESSING

The SP&A word processing system will be used until the book has been edited. Then the book will be typeset. We investigated down-loading from our word processor to the typesetter, but the cost savings, given our equipment, is not worth the effort.

REPRODUCTION

Review copies will be prepared on our copy machine. Final copy will go to a printer for book-quality printing. A high-quality, heavy weight paper with no show-through should be used. Before making a choice, see samples with two-sided printing.

GRAPHIC ARTS

Examples in the book which are supposed to be done by a writer should be done by us. Other illustrations should be done by a graphic artist. The final version also needs paste-up by a graphic artist.

ASSEMBLY

The printer should assemble the book.

Sample Project Writing Guide

The project writing guide on the following pages is the one used to produce the typed version of this book. The typed version used a word processing system, so some of the page format notes have the word processing needs in mind. For example, the guide specifies the left margin for printing the document and describes tabs and text and heading placement in terms of the column position counter.

Only a few of the text and graphic standards are unique for this book. An asterisk indicates these. The remaining standards are part of Sandra Pakin & Associates' corporate style guide.

When you develop the writing guide for your project, use applicable corporate style guides. You may simply refer to the corporate style guide as a source of these standards or, for convenience, you may repeat them in the project writing guide.

The writing guide contains the following sections:
- Sample pages
- Page format notes
- Text standards
- Graphics standards

In project planning, you prepare an overview plan for the entire
project. Then when development begins on a specific document,
such as a user's guide, a long-range strategy report, a
feasibility study, or a brochure, you prepare a detailed plan
for that document by:

o Defining requirements.
o Outlining the content.
o Developing the page format.
o Specifying the schedule and resources.

The result of this planning effort is the document plan.

REQUIREMENTS DEFINITION

For requirements definition, you determine the objectives,
scope, purpose, and audience of the specific document. You write
up this information in a requirements statement for the
document. The requirements statement covers three areas of
information to steer the development of the document:

o   Subject overview
o   Scope and purpose of the document
o   Audience definition

SUBJECT OVERVIEW

The subject overview is a one or two paragraph statement of the
subject prompting the documentation. For a user's guide, this
section is the system overview and includes the purpose of the
system, its general functions, and its processing flow from the
point of view of the intended audience. For a long-range
strategy report, this section is a mission statement. You write
the subject overview to orient yourself and your reviewers to
the subject of the document.

SCOPE AND PURPOSE

The document scope and purpose section amplifies the content
information provided in the project plan. The document scope

CHECKPOINT	DAYS	COMPLETE DATE
Write first draft and develop graphics . .	35	Feb. 19
Type the first draft; assemble review copy.	10	Mar. 5
Review the draft for technical accuracy . .	5	Mar. 12
Rewrite the draft and complete graphcs. . .	20	Apr. 9
Type the rewrite corrections.	5	Apr. 16
Conduct user review	10	Apr. 30
Incorporate user comments	5	May 7
Type the corrections; prepare final draft .	3	May 12
Review final draft	2	May 14
Make final corrections	2	May 18
Print the copies.	10	June 1
Assemble the copies	2	June 3

Figure 5.5 Specifying a development schedule. The schedule
assumes that writing began on January 4 and that no development
work is done on weekends.

Once you know the development schedule, you can prepare the
production control forms for tracking the development of the
document. Chapter 14, "Production Control," explains how to
design these forms.

NUMBER OF COPIES NEEDED

Knowing the number of copies is necessary for ordering supplies
and for specifying the number of copies to be made during
publication. The number can also affect distribution.

To determine the number of copies, start with the total number
of copies required for the initial distribution. To this base
number, add the number of copies required for:

o   Filing and library back-up
o   Complimentary copies
o   Reasonable inventory

To determine the inventory number, consider the life of the
document (one time, one year before revisions) and the new
audience potential (new employees, new users).

DISTRIBUTION REQUIREMENTS

During document planning, you can determine methods for
distributing the material. Some possible distribution methods

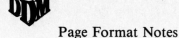

TEXT
1. Text begins in position 15 and continues through position 79.
2. Tabs are set at 19 22 31 40 50 60 70.
3. Headings begin in position 1.

PAGINATION
4. There are no more than 53 lines of text on a page.

LEFT MARGIN
5. Set the left margin to 11 when printing the document.

PAGE NUMBERING
6. a. Draft: Number pages within chapter, as x-y, where x is the chapter number and y is the consecutive page number.
   b. Final: Number pages consecutively throughout the book.
7. Number front matter with lower-case roman numerals.
8. Assign a number to every page.
9. Begin each part and chapter on an odd-numbered page.

HEADER
10. Begin the header text two lines from the top edge of the paper and follow it by four line spaces. The complete header appears as follow:

> Chapter x - Chapter Title

11. The chapter title is flush right.
12. The header does not appear on the first page of a part or a chapter.
13. Separate the footer text from the text by three line spaces. The complete footer appears as follows:

> mm/dd/yy   Sandra Pakin & Associates, Inc.   x-y

PRINTING
14. Use the titan-12 printwheel.

HEADINGS
15. Precede all headings by two line spaces and follow by one line space.
16. The following rules apply for the various levels of all headings:
   • Part or Chapter Heading. The part or chapter heading is all caps and underscored across the width of the page. It is separated from the main subject heading or introductory chapter text by five line spaces.
   • Main Section Heading. A main section heading is all caps and underscored on a line by itself. It begins in position 1.
   • Subject Heading. A subject heading is all caps on a line by itself. It begins in position 1.
   • Topic Heading. A topic heading is initial caps and underscored on a line by itself. It begins in position 1.
   • Minor Heading. A minor heading is initial caps and underscored and is followed immediately by text. It begins in position 15.

FIGURES AND TABLES
17. Figures and tables may begin in position 1 or position 15 and extend through position 78.
18. Separate figures and tables from the text by two line spaces and an underscore at the top. At the bottom have an underscore immediately followed by the figure caption and two line spaces.

TABLE OF CONTENTS   19. The following formats apply:
- Precede main sections by two line spaces. They are all caps and followed by one line space. They begin in position 15.
- Subjects are initial cap and begin in position 17. Single space between subjects.

20. Use periods to extend the contents to position 60.

GLOSSARY   21. Begin term in position 1 and definition in position 15.

INDEX   22. The typed copy will not have an index.

EXAMPLES   23. Begin example text in position 19.

Text Standards

This section contains text standards for the following:
- Abbreviations
- Glossary
- Lists
- Punctuation
- Spelling and capitalization
- Word list for spelling
- Word use

For items not covered by this writing guide, refer to the *University of Chicago Manual of Style (12th edition)*.

Abbreviations
1. Show the full spelling of an abbreviation the first time it is used.
2. Spell out i.e. (that is) and e.g. (for example).
3. Use the symbols % and $ with numbers. Use the words *percent* and *dollars* with spelled out numbers.
4. Avoid using etc. by introducing a list with the words *such as* or by defining what the continuation is.
5. Do not use etc. with a list introduced by *such as, for example,* or any similar expression.
6. Form the plural of an abbreviation by adding *s,* not *'s,* unless there might be confusion.

Glossary
1. Capitalize terms in the glossary and index only if they are ordinarily capitalized.
2. Definition of an abbreviation is its spelled out form. Put the definition under the spelled out form.
3. Alphabetize the glossary word by word.

Lists

BULLETS VS. NUMBERS   1. Prefer bullets. Use numbers only when the sequence of items is important.

FORMAT   2. Start bullets in position 15. Begin text in position 18.

3. Numbered lists
   a. Where the list has more than nine items, begin digits 1-9 in position 16. Begin numbers of 10 or more in position 15. Begin text in position 18.
   b. Where the list has fewer than ten items, begin numbers in position 15 and text in position 18.

4. If the text for the item is longer than a line, begin each succeeding line in position 18.

SPACING   5. If the list items do not extend past column 60, single space the items. Otherwise, doublespace the list items.

PUNCTUATING LISTS   6. End all list items that include a verb or a verbal (participle, gerund, or infinitive) with a period or a question mark. Do not punctuate simple lists.

7. If any item in a list is punctuated, punctuate all items in the list.

8. No list item should end with a comma, a semicolon, or the words *and* or *or*.

9. Follow a lead-in term or phrase by a period and two spaces, then the text. Do not use a dash.

CAPITALIZING LISTS 10. Begin each bullet item with a capital. Lower-case all other words unless they would ordinarily be capitalized.

CONSISTENCY 11. Structure all items within a list similarly.

INTRODUCING A LIST 12. Every list should be introduced with a sentence or phrase.

13. The sentence or phrase that introduces a list should end with a period or a colon. The final word in the introductory phrase should not be *a* or *the*.

SUBLIST 14. Use a hyphen or numbers for the sublist of a bulleted item.

15. Use a bullet or a lower-case alphabetic character for the sublist of a numbered item.

Punctuation
DASHES 1. Represent a dash as two hyphens (--). Use one space before and after the dash.

2. A dash should not begin a line.

QUOTATION MARKS 3. Do not put terms being defined within quotation marks. Underscore them instead.

4. Use quotation marks when referring to a part, chapter, or section title.

*5. Do not use quotation marks for the name of a task.

6. Use a comma after the next-to-last item in a series.

*7. Use commas to set off the name of a task or a chapter in a reference, such as Task 3, Plan Document Content, or Chapter 6, "Review Management."

Spelling and Capitalization
STANDARD DICTIONARY 1. Use *Webster's Collegiate Dictionary* for spelling.

2. Use *Webster's Third International Dictionary* for words not found in the collegiate.

NUMBERS 3. Spell out integral numbers from zero through ten *unless:*
   - Space is limited, as in a table.
   - Referring to something identified by a number.
   - Expressing a range when the high number is over ten.

4. Use figures for nonintegers and numbers greater than ten *unless* the number begins a sentence.

CAPITALIZATION *5. Do not capitalize DDM outputs, such as project writing guide, project plan.

*6. Capitalize the specific name of a task, such as Plan Documentation Project. Lower-case general references, such as project planning.

7. Capitalize step, task, part, figure, or chapter when it is followed by a number, such as Task 4.

8. Lower-case general department names, such as graphic arts, accounting, print shop.

*Word List

Capitalization and spelling for special words in this book:

callout (adj, n)	logon (adj)	paste up (v)
call out (v)	log on (v)	playscript
cross-reference list	mark-up (n)	project plan
development control form	mark up (v)	project writing guide
distribution list	offline	sign-off (adj)
document plan	online	sign off (v)
field test	on-site	visual table of contents
figure control list	paste-up (n)	word processing log

™ of Sandra Pakin & Associates, Inc.

Word Use	1.	**USE**	**NOT**
		data is	data are
		*edit	copy edit
		*headings	headlines
		if	if...then
		press	depress
		shows *or*	
		summarizes *or*	overviews
		lists	
		to	in order to
		*typist	word processing operator
		*word processing	text processing

*2. *Text,* not *copy,* when referring to the content of a document.

3. Do not use *input* as a verb.

*4. Use *medium* as the singular of *media.*

5. Use *appendixes, matrixes,* and *indexes* as the plurals of *appendix, matrix,* and *index,* respectively.

6. Do not use contractions.

*7. *Typed,* not *printed,* if the text comes from a word processing system.

8. *Type,* not *enter,* for word processing input.

9. Use pronoun *he (him, his)* throughout, even for secretaries, typists, clerks.

Graphics Standards

This section contains graphics standards for the following:
- Figure format
- Illustrations
- Table format

Figure Format

CAPTIONS
1. Begin all figure captions with a figure number.
2. Number figures within chapter as x.y, where x is the chapter number and y is the sequential figure number.
3. Have two spaces between the figure number and the caption.
4. The figure caption text is initial cap only, unless a term would normally be capitalized.
5. No punctuation follows a figure caption, unless it is followed by an explanatory sentence or two.
6. Figure captions should be shorter than a line. Use an explanatory sentence following the caption if necessary.
7. If a figure extends more than one page, repeat the figure number and caption followed by (page x of y). The caption must be the same.

Illustrations

1. Box in all example pages to show they are examples.
2. Do not show blank forms. Always have example data.
*3. Make the explanation of callout items part of the figure.
4. Use hand-printing whenever the reader would normally print, such as in filling out a production control form.
*5. Use reverse numbers (white-on-black) for callouts.
*6. Use Lectratone LT-900 for shading.

Table Format

1. Make column headings all caps.
2. Underscore between sections of a table. Doublespace before and after the underscore.

3. Indent the first heading and the first column of text two spaces to allow room to draw the vertical line. Three spaces should separate columns so a vertical line can be drawn. Text in the final column should end in position 78.
4. Draw vertical lines separating the columns by hand.
5. If a table continues to the next page, repeat the table headings.
6. Treat tables like figures and give figure numbers and captions.

Appendix C
Additional Reading on Writing Topics

English is constantly changing and evolving through the choices writers and speakers make among various words and constructions in the language. This dynamic quality of language often makes it difficult to determine what is correct.

Correct English usage, in fact, does not depend upon fixed rules but on what is acceptable to discerning language users. As a result, many language experts write books on usage. Each of the following books is an excellent reference for MIS writers. Each offers worthwhile suggestions for simplifying your language.

Bernstein, Theodore M. *Watch Your Language.* New York: Atheneum, 1979.

Evans, Bergen, and Evans, Cornelia. *A Dictionary of Contemporary American Usage.* New York: Random House, 1957.

Flesch, Rudolph. *The ABC of Style: A Guide to Plain English.* New York: Harper & Row, 1964.

Morris, William, and Morris, Mary. *Harper Dictionary of Contemporary Usage.* New York: Harper & Row, 1975.

Strunk, William Jr., and White, E.B. *The Elements of Style.* 3rd ed. New York: Macmillan, 1979.

 **Glossary**

audience. Readers of the document. Knowing the audience of a document helps you develop an appropriate approach and structure for it.

back matter. Publishing term to identify those portions of a book or manual that come after the main content. Includes appendixes, bibliography, glossary of terms, and index. *See also* front matter.

callout. Graphic device for calling attention to features of a figure or illustration. Callouts may be descriptive phrases or numbers or letters that are keyed to a text discussion.

control information. Means of helping a reader locate and identify pages in a manual. Control information may include document identification, page number, date, corporate logo, software family logo, section and subject title headers or footers, and word processing document or file number.

document development. Writing, reviewing, illustrating and producing a document.

development control form. Form for tracking document through its development.

development scenario. Tasks and activities needed to develop a specific document. The activities listed in the development scenario represent development checkpoints, when the material changes hands — when it goes to review, to typing, to testing, back to you for further development.

distribution list. Names of people or offices who should receive the published document.

document plan. Design specification for a specific document. It includes requirements statement, outline, page format, schedule, and resources.

DDM. Documentation Development Methodology.

Documentation Development Methodology. Structured approach for developing all types of formal written materials. It consists of ten tasks, beginning with planning and ending with publication of the document.

draft. Interim version of a document.

editorial review. Review of a document to check for textual consistency, grammatical accuracy, and conformity with standards.

extended outline. Detailed outline of a document that specifies the content for each topic. *See also* topic outline.

field test. Preliminary release of a draft of a document for use by a typical audience in the actual work situation.

figure control list. Control form for tracking the preparation of figures and illustrations.

first draft. Writer's first attempt to write the document. The first draft is distributed for technical review before time is spent polishing the writing style.

final draft. Complete draft with all corrections made. It includes text, graphics pasted down in place, front matter, and back matter.

footer. Control information found at the bottom of a page, such as a chapter title, date, or page number.

format. Structure for the arrangment of elements of all pages of all documents associated with a project. *See also* layout.

front matter. Publishing term for the part of a book or manual that comes before the main content. Front matter may include abstract, preface, table of contents, illustration list, and acknowledgments. *See also* back matter.

glossary. Collection of terms used in a document and their definitions.

graphic arts. In this book, the support service that prepares figures and illustrations.

header. Control information that appears at the top of each page, such as corporate logo, section title, or page number.

history file. Papers taken from the project file that provide background information on the project. *See also* project file, update file.

illustration list. List of each figure in a book or manual and its page number. The illustration list usually follows the master table of contents.

index. Alphabetic arrangement of topics in a book or manual.

layout. Way elements are arranged on a specific page. *See also* format.

legibility. Mechanical ease with which material can be read. Factors that affect legibility include type size and style, line length, paper, and ink.

module. Content unit of information on a single function or for a single audience.

media. Forms of documents, such as manuals, brochures, reference cards, newsletters.

outline. *See* extended outline, topic outline.

page format: *See* format.

production. Activities associated with page preparation, reproduction, and assembly of a document.

production control. Activities associated with tracking document development and working with support services to type the material, prepare figures, order supplies, and reproduce copies.

project file. Collection point for all development information and drafts of a document.

project plan. Design specification for an entire documentation project. It includes project design and development requirements.

project writing guide. Collection of standards and guidelines associated with the textual and graphic development of documents in the project.

proofreading. Matching *word for word* the submitted copy of a document to that received from word processing or the typesetter. No editorial changes or rewriting should be done during proofreading.

publication. Preparation of the document for distribution.

purchasing. In this book, the support service responsible for ordering such supplies as binders, tabs, and paper.

readability. Ease with which a document can be read and understood. Covers such items as vocabulary, sentence structure, and sentence length.

reader's comment form. Sheet included in a manual that solicits corrections and comments from the reader.

referenceability. Ease with which information can be located in a book or manual. *See also* reference aids.

reference aids. Components of a book or manual that help a reader locate information. Common reference aids are table of contents, index, headings, tabs.

reproduction services. In this book, the support service responsible for duplicating the document, such as by office copier or by offset printing.

support services. Anyone who provides help in publishing the document. Typical support services are word processing, reproduction, graphic arts, and purchasing.

technical review. Review of a draft for content accuracy and completeness.

topic outline. Outline of a document showing how information is to be organized.

typist. In this book, the person who uses the word processing equipment — regardless of the type of equipment or the person's job title.

typeset. Prepare the text portion of the document by setting type. In typesetting, a variety of type fonts is available in various sizes. Typeset material is proportionally spaced and may be right-justified.

update file. Information from the project file that is needed when the document is being updated.

user review. Review of a draft by users for the usefulness of the instructions in their business operations, the appropriateness of the language and examples, and the readability of the material.

visual table of contents. Arrangement of the main topics of a document in a hierarchy chart, similar to an organization chart.

VTOC. Visual table of contents.

white space. Blank areas on a page, such as the margins.

word processing. In this book, the support service responsible for the typed preparation of a draft.

word processing log. Control form for keeping track of material given to and received from the word processing service.

DDM Index

™ of Sandra Pakin & Associates, Inc.

of Sandra Pakin & Associates, Inc.

Afterword

Sandra Pakin & Associates, Inc. (SP&A) is the nation's foremost consulting firm devoted exclusively to planning, developing, and teaching computer documentation. Founded in 1976, SP&A has completed successful documentation planning and development engagements with Fortune 500 companies, Fortune 50 banking, insurance, and retail companies, and Big Eight accounting firms, as well as hardware and software vendors in the Datamation 100. Headquartered in Chicago, Illinois, the firm works with clients throughout the United States.

SP&A's engagements include:
- Customization and installation of the DDM.
- Strategic documentation planning for end users and hardware-software vendors.
- Help screen and online tutorial development.
- Operator's and user's guides for online systems.
- MIS long-range strategy reports.
- Product descriptions and other marketing materials.
- Data center operations manuals.
- System development methodologies.
- Development standards.
- Operating standards.

Experienced in all aspects of documentation development, SP&A's consultants are recognized experts in the field. The staff has presented talks and papers for numerous professional and technical organizations, including:
- Association for Computing Machinery (ACM)
- Association of System Managers (ASM)
- Chicago Area Standards Exchange (CASE)
- Data Processing Management Association (DPMA)
- EDP Auditors Association
- Independent Computer Consultants Association (ICCA)
- International Technical Communications Conference (ITCC)
- National Conference on Productivity in Information Systems
- SHARE
- Society for Technical Communications (STC)

SP&A is dedicated to improving documentation skills in the data processing industry. SP&A publishes FOLIO, an award-winning quarterly journal devoted to the development of quality documentation. In addition, SP&A has developed a unique customized documentation training course to help data processing professionals improve their documentation skills. The training course and this book are based on SP&A's Documentation Development Methodology (DDM).

229

Return to:

Sandra Pakin & Associates, Inc.
Publications Division
6007 N. Sheridan Road
Chicago, Illinois 60660

YOUR COMMENTS PLEASE...

Your comments can help us improve the usefulness of *DDM: The Documentation Development Methodology.* They will be carefully reviewed.

Possible topics for comment include *clarity, questions not answered, accuracy, organization, figures, examples.*

Thank you for your cooperation.

Page   Comment

I would like a reply:

Name_____   Phone (   ) -_____

Address_____

City, State, Zip_____